CONSCIOUS **COLLECTIVE**

An Aim for Awareness

Joseph P. Kauffman,

Conscious Collective, LLC

http://www.conscious-collective.com

Also Available on Amazon Kindle

Dedication

Our fast-paced society makes it difficult to understand the reality of our situation. The people are oppressed and manipulated by governments, corporations, banks, and many other wealthy institutions, and our way of life ignores the importance of health and sustainability in supporting our survival. Most people go through life working a job or going to school or doing whatever they feel is necessary, never taking the time to realize how they are contributing to the destruction of Earth's resources. This book is dedicated to those who seek a better understanding of what it means to be a human being on planet Earth, and to everyone who actually cares to make a difference in our society. Furthermore, I dedicate this book to all of the people who have changed my life. To every person I have come in contact with who has helped me become the person that I am today. My family, friends, and every scientist, philosopher, activist, musician, or author who has taught me to question things, and to live life based on what I think is morally right. Most importantly, I dedicate this book to you, the reader, with hopes that you learn from this book to contribute to the overall good of humanity. Thank you for taking the time to read this.

Table of Contents

Introduction

The reason that I have written this book is because I am fed up with the current situation of the world. We have the knowledge, the resources, and the technology to provide a society that benefits all of humanity, yet we still live in a world where material wealth and self-interest are the motives for success. Nothing is how it should be.

> *"Just look at us. Everything is backwards, everything is upside down. Doctors destroy health, lawyers destroy justice, psychiatrists destroy minds, scientists destroy truth, major media destroys information, religions destroy spirituality and governments destroy freedom."*
>
> *– Michael Ellner*

What is even more troubling is the fact that the majority of people are completely unaware of the condition that our society is in. They believe whatever they can to make sense of our diseased culture and continue living their lives based on these delusional belief systems. I cannot continue participating in a sick society, without knowing I did all that I could to fix it.

I am not a scientist, philosopher, or writer, at least not in the eyes of our culture. I have no degree from a prestigious university. I am simply a human being who has realized the extent to which our society has been conditioned, controlled, and oppressed to serve the interests of the people in power, and how ignorance of this fact has resulted in environmental pollution and the decline of human health on a global scale. Our potential is limited by people who couldn't care less about the well being of human life, the life of animals, or the planet as a whole.

The wealthy class controls the majority of people, but we must also take responsibility for our own actions. We have allowed ourselves to conform to a completely unnatural way of life, and as a result our planet is suffering. Whatever damage we do to the planet, we do to ourselves. We depend on the resources that we pollute every day. To put an end to environmental pollution, we need to stop supporting the companies that participate in these practices, and develop more sustainable and healthy options for harvesting resources.

I may not be the most qualified person to write this book, but I have a strong desire to improve the state of our society and have been exposed to information that every human being needs to know. We can no longer afford to lead such ignorant lifestyles. I have done my best to provide the necessary knowledge for understanding our current situation, and by all means I do not think that I have all the answers. But I do believe that the information in this book can benefit anyone who reads it, and will serve as a platform from which people can discover topics for doing their own research.

The world as we know it is rapidly changing. As everything around us grows more chaotic, it is clear that humanity is facing the next step in human evolution. Over the past 200 years, since the dawn of the industrial revolution, our unconscious acts have had a major effect on our environment. As global temperatures, carbon emissions, and levels of pollution and animal extinction rise, it is obvious that it is time for change. Unless humanity makes a drastic change in our way of life, the Earth will continue to grow more hazardous, and less habitable.

The purpose of this book is to draw attention to the ongoing problems that face humanity, and to provide solutions. While reading this book, I ask that you keep an open mind, hold aside any previously held beliefs that you may have, and try to see the seriousness of the problems addressed. Do not just read this book; absorb the information that is presented. I also ask that with the knowledge you gain from this book, to please inform all of your friends, family, colleagues, acquaintances, etc. There is still hope for humanity, but unless every individual learns to work together, a future for the people of planet Earth is nothing but a dream.

"The quicker we all realize that we've been taught how to live by people that were operating on the momentum of an ignorant past, the quicker we can move to a global ethic of community that doesn't value invented borders or the monopolization of natural resources, but rather the goal of a happier, more loving humanity."

– Joe Rogan

Part I
Environmental Destruction

Chapter 1. The Human Virus

"We have the money, the power, the medical understanding, the scientific know-how, the love and the community to produce a kind of human paradise. But we are led by the least among us—the least intelligent, the least noble, the least visionary."

– Terrance McKenna

Human beings have become a virus to planet Earth. Our way of life consists of constant pollution of natural resources, violence between nations, oppression of populations, torturing of animals, and the destruction of our own health and wellness. Our society is not sustainable and the people in control have no interest in the well being of the people or the planet.

If we do not change our way of life, and fast, we will destroy ourselves by continuing to pollute the environment that sustains us, abusing natural resources, poisoning our food supply, destroying large ecosystems, contaminating the air, and perpetuating climate change.

A 2012 United Nations report states that a global population growth from 7 billion to nearly 9 billion is expected by 2040; demands for resources will rise exponentially. By 2030, demands for food are expected to rise by 50%, energy by 45%, and water by 30%. We are currently depleting natural resources 50% faster than the planet can renew. At this rate, it is estimated that we will need three more planet Earths to keep up with resource needs as they are today.[1]

Clearly, our current system is not sustainable. We are at a critical time in our planet's history where we are required to decide whether we want to change our values, adopt a more positive, intelligent, peaceful, healthy, sustainable and loving society, and work together as one planet to survive against the struggles of nature, or continue on the path that we are on, leading to more war, famine, poverty, illness, environmental pollution, and perhaps the extinction of our species and many others, an event that many are referring to as the sixth mass extinction.

Mass extinctions are periods in Earth's history when unusually large numbers of species die out simultaneously or within a limited time frame. The most severe occurred at the end of the Permian period (299 to 251 million years ago) when 96% of all species perished.

Our planet is now in the midst of its sixth mass extinction of plants and animals. We're currently experiencing the worst epidemic of species die-offs since the loss of the dinosaurs 65 million years ago, with literally dozens of species going extinct every day. At this rate, the future for life on earth is looking grim, with as many as 30 to 50 percent of all species possibly heading toward extinction by mid-century.[2]

Unlike past mass extinctions however, caused by events like volcanic eruptions, asteroid strikes, and natural climate shifts, the current crisis is almost entirely caused by humans. In fact, 99 percent of currently

---

[1] http://www.un.org/en/development/desa/news/population/un-report-world-population-projected-to-reach-9-6-billion-by-2050.html

[2] http://www.biologicaldiversity.org/programs/biodiversity/elements_of_biodiversity/extinction_crisis/

threatened species are at risk from human activities, mainly those driving habitat loss, introduction of exotic species, and global warming. Because the rate of change in our biosphere is increasing, and because every species' extinction potentially leads to the extinction of others bound to that species in an intricate ecological web, numbers of extinctions are likely to increase in the coming decades as ecosystems unravel.

Some of the problems that are causing the environmental disasters we are experiencing are easy to fix, while others are more difficult. Ultimately, what humanity needs to accomplish is a dramatic change in our lifestyle. We need to change the way we view the world and the way we interact with it. We must also encourage corporations, governments, and politicians to realize the threat they pose to our environment and change the way they obtain and manage natural resources.

The current practices of distributing resources are not sustainable and will continue to harm the environment if we do not evolve our methods into procedures that are more practical based on the needs of today's society.

Chapter 2. The Biosphere

The biosphere is made up of the parts of Earth where life exists. The biosphere extends from the deepest root systems of trees, to the dark environment of ocean trenches, to lush rain forests and high mountaintops.

Scientists describe the Earth in terms of spheres. The solid surface layer of the Earth is the lithosphere. The atmosphere is the layer of air that stretches above the lithosphere. The Earth's water—on the surface, in the ground, and in the air—makes up the hydrosphere.

Since life exists on the ground, in the air, and in the water, the biosphere overlaps all of these spheres. Although the biosphere measures about 20 kilometers (12 miles) from top to bottom, almost all life exists between about 500 meters (1,640 feet) below the ocean's surface to about 6 kilometers (3.75 miles) above sea level.[3]

The biosphere, along with Earth's other spheres, is compromised by the pollution driven by human activity. The following chapters address some of the critical forms of pollution that humanity must transform in order to prevent a mass extinction.

[3] nationalgeographic.com

Chapter 3. Deforestation

Deforestation is the conversion of forested areas to non-forest land for uses such as arable fields, pastures, urban use, logged areas, or wasteland. Deforestation can also be seen as removal of forests leading to several imbalances ecologically and environmentally and results in declines in habitat and biodiversity.[4]

Forests are cut down for many reasons, but most of them are related to money or to people's need to provide for their families. The biggest driver of deforestation is agriculture. Farmers cut forests to provide more room for planting crops or grazing livestock. Often many small farmers will each clear a few acres to feed their families by cutting down trees and burning them in a process known as "slash and burn" agriculture.

Logging operations, which provide the world's wood and paper products, also cut countless trees each year. Loggers, some of them acting illegally, also build roads to access more and more remote forests—which leads to further deforestation. Forests are also cut as a result of growing urban sprawl.

Trees play a critical role in absorbing the greenhouse gases that fuel global warming. Fewer forests mean larger amounts of greenhouse gases entering the atmosphere—and increased speed and severity of global warming.

---

[4] http://environment.nationalgeographic.com/environment/global-warming/deforestation-overview/

The quickest solution to deforestation would be to simply stop cutting down trees, or to replace the use of trees with a more sustainable resource like hemp. Though deforestation rates have slowed a bit in recent years, financial realities make this unlikely to occur.

A more workable solution is to carefully manage forest resources by eliminating clear-cutting to make sure that forest environments remain intact.[5]

---

[5] http://www.conserve-energy-future.com/various-deforestation-facts.php

Chapter 4. Air Pollution

Air pollution has become a growing threat to our health and welfare because of the ever-increasing emissions of air contaminants into our never-increasing atmosphere. An average adult requires 30 pounds of air each day, compared to about 2.65 pounds of food and 4.5 pounds of water; therefore, the cleanliness of our air should be as important to us as the cleanliness of our food and water.[6]

Earth's atmosphere is about 300 miles (480 km) thick, but most of it is within 10 miles (16 km) of the surface. Air pressure decreases with altitude. At sea level, air pressure is about 14.7 pounds per square inch (PSI) (1 kg per square centimeter).[7]

There have always been many natural sources of air pollution. Ash from volcanic eruptions, salt particles from breaking waves, pollen and spores released by plants, smoke from forest fires, and windblown dust are all examples of natural air pollution. However, from the time humans have been on Earth they have added to the intensity of these natural pollutants, particularly smoke and dust. With the discovery of fire came many accidental as well as intentional burnings. Even today forest fires are used to clear land for agriculture purposes.

The Industrial Revolution brought with it a radical increase in air pollution. Beyond accelerating natural pollutants, people found many new ways to pollute the air. The rapid increase in air pollution was not always

[6] Foundations of Earth Science [5th Edition]

[7] space.com

viewed with alarm. Chimneys belching smoke used to be a sign of growth and prosperity.

When cars burn gasoline, they emit pollutants. Gasoline fumes escape into the air even when we pump gasoline into our fuel tanks. There are three major pollutants that come from cars. A car emits carbon monoxide when the carbon in fuel doesn't burn completely. A car's exhaust emits hydrocarbons, a toxic compound of hydrogen and carbon. When fuel burns, nitrogen and oxygen react with each other and form nitrogen oxides. According to the EPA, motor vehicles collectively cause 75% of carbon monoxide pollution in the U.S.[8]

Industrial factories emit another large portion of air pollutants into our atmosphere. When smoke floats toward the sky it does not disappear. It stays in our atmosphere, affecting the air that we breathe. Many things that we use today pollute the air, including aerosol containers, industrial production, transportation, and many others. If we do not find ways to reduce the amount of pollutants we create, it will have serious effects in the near future.

---

[8] http://www3.epa.gov/airquality/peg_caa/carstrucks.html

Chapter 5. Water Pollution

As a result of our society's negative cycles of production and consumption, we have polluted much of the Earth's air along with much of its water. Water is the most common substance on Earth; it makes up nearly 71% of the planet. The surface area of the Earth is about 197 million square miles (510 million square km). Of that, 139 million square miles (360 million square km) are oceans, while the remaining 58 million square miles (150 million square km) is land. Water is always on the move from ocean to land and back again. Every species comes from water and needs water to survive. The human body is also roughly 71% water. Without water life would not be possible.[9]

The Pacific Ocean is home to something known as the Great Pacific Garbage Patch, which is also known to the European Commission as the "World's Largest Landfill." An estimated 3.5 million tons of concentrated marine debris reside in this landfill that are the result of whirling currents in the Pacific Ocean that pull trash and pollution into the ocean. The landfill's area is the size of Europe, or 3.45 million square km.[10] Fourteen billion pounds of garbage are dumped into the ocean every year. Most of it is plastic.

The Great Pacific Garbage Patch is also called the Pacific trash vortex; it spans waters from the West Coast of North America to Japan. The patch actually comprises the Eastern Garbage Patch, located near Japan, and the

---

[9] https://en.wikipedia.org/wiki/Earth

[10] http://education.nationalgeographic.org/encyclopedia/great-pacific-garbage-patch/

Western Garbage Patch, located between the U.S. states of Hawaii and California.

These areas of spinning debris are linked together by the North Pacific Subtropical Convergence Zone, located a few hundred kilometers north of Hawaii. This convergence zone is where warm water from the South Pacific meets up with cooler water from the Arctic. The zone acts like a highway that moves debris from one patch to another.[11]

The entire Great Pacific Garbage Patch is bounded by the North Pacific Subtropical Gyre. An ocean gyre is a system of circular ocean currents formed by the Earth's wind patterns and the forces created by the rotation of the planet. The North Pacific Subtropical Gyre is created by the interaction of the California, North Equatorial, Kuroshiro, and North Pacific currents. These four currents move in a clockwise direction around an area of 20 million square km (7.7 million square miles).

The area in the center of a gyre tends to be very calm and stable. The circular motion of the gyre draws debris into this stable center, where it becomes trapped. A plastic water bottle discarded off the coast of California, for instance, takes the California Current south toward Mexico. There, it may catch the North Equatorial Current, which crosses the vast Pacific. Near the coast of Japan, the bottle may travel north on the powerful Kuroshiro Current. Finally, the bottle travels westward on the North Pacific Current. The gently rolling vortexes of the Eastern and Western Garbage Patches gradually draw in the bottle.

Fish and marine life comprise the food chain in the Pacific Ocean, helping to maintain life's natural balance and keep marine species from

[11] http://marinedebris.noaa.gov/info/patch.html

becoming extinct. Due to the high amount of plastic in the Pacific Ocean, the fish species also have been affected. Fish ingest an estimated 12,000 to 24,000 tons of plastic per year in the Pacific Ocean, according to research from the University of California San Diego's Scripps Institution of Oceanography. Institute researchers collected 141 fishes of 27 species and found that 9.2 percent of the fish had small bits of plastic debris in their stomachs.[12] The continual consumption of plastic not only effects the fish but the whole food chain – the animals that eat those fish, including sharks, whales, dolphins, and humans.

The amount of pollution we have dumped in the sea has resulted in the acidification of ocean water. The ocean makes up roughly 70% of the planet; living on land, we fail to recognize the importance of our ocean and the marine life that inhabit it. Ocean acidification is making phytoplankton toxic, which is bad news for the organisms that depend on them as a source of food and oxygen. Phytoplankton generates a large portion of the world's O_2. If they're out of balance, the rest of life on Earth is going to be out of balance.

When phytoplankton, the single-celled organisms that constitute the very foundation of the marine food web turn toxic, their toxins often concentrate in the shellfish and many other marine species that feed on them. Ocean acidification will dangerously alter these microscopic plants, which nourish a menagerie of sea creatures and produce up to 60% of the Earth's oxygen.[13]

---

[12] https://scripps.ucsd.edu/news/1928

[13] http://www.fondriest.com/environmental-measurements/parameters/water-quality/algae-phytoplankton-chlorophyll/

One of the biggest sources of water pollution is called nonpoint source pollution, which occurs as a result of runoff. Nonpoint source pollution includes many small sources, like septic tanks, cars, trucks, and boats, plus larger sources, such as farms, ranches, and forest areas. Millions of motor vehicle engines drop small amounts of oil each day onto roads and parking lots. Much of this, too, makes its way to the sea. When large tracts of land are plowed, the exposed soil can erode during rainstorms. Much of this runoff flows to the sea, carrying with it agricultural fertilizers and pesticides.

Many of our lakes and rivers are polluted as well. The Mississippi River carries an estimated 1.5 million metric tons of nitrogen pollution into the Gulf of Mexico each year, creating a "dead zone" in the Gulf each summer about the size of New Jersey. Approximately 40% of the lakes in America are too polluted for fishing, aquatic life, or swimming. Each year, 1.2 trillion gallons of untreated sewage, storm water, and industrial waste are dumped into U.S. waters.[14]

Water is meant to flow naturally. Originally, it starts in oceans and evaporates to clouds, rains in to mountains and rivers, and flows from rivers back to the ocean to complete what is known as the hydrologic cycle or the rain cycle. This cycle is the only natural water cycle that exists on Earth. It is the cycle that creates a living web of life on the planet. When it flows into our homes, it does not flow naturally. It moves through pipes at angles and straight lines, restricting its natural flow.

Most cities work on a closed-loop system, where water is recycled continually. The water passes through aggressive chemical purification, and

---

[14] http://www.livescience.com/22728-pollution-facts.html

powerful filters, then returns to our homes, permanently effected by the chemicals it was subjected to. Our tap water is contaminated with chlorine, fluoride, arsenic, lead, copper, mercury, and other chemicals and pesticides.[15] This type of chemical exposure is not natural and it is not only affecting our water but it is affecting our health.

Fukushima

Another tragedy that has greatly contributed to the pollution of the planet is the radioactive water leak at the Fukushima-Daiichi Nuclear Plant in Japan. On March 11, 2011 a 9.0 magnitude earthquake hit Sendai, Japan sending a massive tsunami crashing into the Fukushima-Daiichi nuclear power plant, destroying cooling pumps located on the beach. As a result, the nuclear furnace inside the crippled plant overheated, leading to a meltdown. Basically, the interior of the reactor got so hot that its fuel rods melted through its metal container, through the concrete "safety net" below, and is now in the ground under the power plant. This super-hot material is now in contact with groundwater and seawater, producing radioactive steam and ocean pollution (300 tons/day).

Over 100,000 Japanese citizens were evicted from their land, never to return home and praying they don't develop cancers or mutations like those in Chernobyl did. Within the first four days following the tsunami, three separate explosions released massive amounts of radioactive fallout worldwide, with the majority depositing (by way of rain) over Tokyo, the United States of America, and the Pacific Ocean. The worst part: TEPCO and

---

[15] http://freshlysqueezedwater.org.uk/waterarticle_watercontent.php

the Japanese government did not admit a meltdown had occurred for two months! Several years later, and Fukushima-Daiichi is still raining death on land, sea, and air and the media blackout continues.[16] [17] [18]

This is not the first time radioactive waste has been dumped into the ocean. A British nuclear fuels plant has repeatedly released radioactive waste into the Irish Sea; a French nuclear reprocessing plant has discharged similar waste into the English Channel; and for decades, the Soviets dumped large quantities of radioactive material into the Arctic Ocean, Kara Sea, and Barents Sea. That radioactive material included reactors from at least 16 Soviet nuclear-powered submarines and icebreakers, and large amounts of liquid and solid nuclear waste from USSR military bases and weapons plants.

Still, there has never been an event as severe as the Fukushima disaster, with millions of tons of radioactive water leaking into the Pacific Ocean, affecting the marine life and inevitably the planet as a whole. Officials are still struggling to clean up after the disaster. This tragic event has proven how much impact humans really have on the planet.[19]

Scientist are unsure of whether it is because of Fukushima, ocean acidification, pollution, or perhaps a combination of all of humanity's negative interactions with the ocean, but marine life in the Pacific Ocean is dying at an alarming rate. Massive numbers of starfish, Bluefin tuna,

---

[16] http://climateviewer.com/2013/10/22/ten-years-of-fukushima-radiation-crossing-the-pacific-ocean/

[17] http://www.nbcnews.com/news/world/radioactive-fukushima-water-leak-was-unreported-months-official-n312396

[18] http://www.rt.com/news/255157-fukushima-radioactive-water-leak/

[19] http://www.globalresearch.ca/fukushima-radioactivity-in-the-pacific-ocean-diluted-but-far-from-harmless/5360752

sardines, anchovies, herring, oysters, salmon, marine mammals, and marine birds are dying, and experts are puzzled.[20]

The animals that are dying are part of a natural web of life, in which all organisms play their role in maintaining the ocean's ecosystems. We cannot expect this event not to have a dramatic effect on the planet.

Fracking

Fracking is yet another form of pollution caused by humans. Fracking, also called "hydraulic fracturing," is a destructive process that corporations like Halliburton, BP and ExxonMobil use to extract natural gas and oil from rock that lies deep underground. They drill a deep well and inject millions of gallons of toxic fracking fluid – a mix of water, sand and harsh chemicals — at a high enough pressure to fracture the rock and release the oil or gas.

The entire process of fracking — from drilling a well to transporting waste — endangers our water and the health of our communities. Some people who live near fracking sites have become seriously ill from drinking contaminated water. Others can light their tap on fire due to the amount of methane in their water. The oil and gas industry isn't required to disclose the chemicals they use in the fracking process, but many are known endocrine disruptors and carcinogens. Communities with fracking have seen declines in property values, increases in crime, and losses in local tourism and agriculture. Methane, a potent greenhouse gas that contributes to climate change, leaks from fracking industry sites.[21]

---

[20] http://www.globalresearch.ca/the-ocean-is-dying-marine-and-animal-life-die-offs-california-coast/5451836

[21] http://www.foodandwaterwatch.org/water/fracking/

Fracking is exempt from major environmental laws, including the Safe Drinking Water Act, and spills and accidents are far too common. Oil spills have dramatically affected the ocean and marine life. Following the explosion and sinking of the Deepwater Horizon oil rig, a sea-floor oil gusher flowed for 87 days, until it was capped on 15 July 2010. The US Government estimated the total discharge at 4.9 million barrels (210 million US gal; 780,000 m3). After several failed efforts to contain the flow, the well was declared sealed on 19 September 2010. Some reports indicate the well site continues to leak.[22]

The fact is that humans have become a virus to the Earth. Our way of life is destroying the planet. Keep in mind that this is the only planet we know of that can sustain our species. We do not have another one to go to. It is our responsibility to take care of the planet so that it can take care of us.

Not only have we polluted the air, soil, rivers, lakes, and oceans, but the majority of food that we eat is extremely toxic as well, and the methods we use to produce this toxic food supply are the causes of most other environmental disasters.

[22] http://www.nola.com/environment/index.ssf/2015/03/bp_spill_posing_ongoing_threat.html

Chapter 6. The Modern Food Industry

The industrial food system began with fast food restaurants. In the 1940s, the McDonald brothers created a very successful drive-in restaurant. To cut costs, they fired many of the employees and reduced the amount of items on their menu. Then they had the revolutionary idea of bringing the factory system to the back of the kitchen. They trained each worker to do one thing again and again, allowing them to be paid a low wage, and become easily replaceable. The food was made fast, tasted good, and was very cheap. The McDonald's fast food business became a huge success.[23]

McDonald's is the largest purchaser of ground beef in the United States. Since they want all of their burgers to taste the same, they have drastically changed the way that beef is produced. They are also the largest purchaser of potatoes and one of the largest purchasers of pork, chicken, tomatoes, and even apples.[24] These big fast food chains want big suppliers, and now there are a handful of companies that basically control our food system.

Think of how many fast food chains exist in the United States alone. Each one of those restaurants needs a large supply of beef, chicken, pork, corn, potatoes, lettuce, tomatoes, cheese, milk, and other food products. To keep up with the demand, they need large corporations to supply them

---

[23] https://en.wikipedia.org/wiki/History_of_McDonald's
[24] https://www.stopcorporateabuse.org/our-food-system

with enough food. When producers focus on benefitting business and industry, they lose their focus on benefitting our health.

In the 1970s, the top five beef packers controlled about 25% of the market.[25] Today, the top four control over 80% of the market.[26] The same thing is happening with pork and other food products. Even if you do not eat at a fast food restaurant, the same companies now produce the majority of food products that are sold in grocery stores.

The fast food industry also completely changed the way that animals are raised. Chickens are now raised and slaughtered in half the time they were 50 years ago, but are also twice the size.[27] The animals are born in a slaughterhouse, overfed to the point where they cannot move, then butchered to become food for us. Sometimes the animals never even see the light of day in their lifetime. Not only is this extremely cruel to the animals, but it has a large impact on human health as well.

Humans depend on the nutrients that food provides us with. Animals provide us with nutrients because the food that they eat gives them nutrients, and we eat them, consuming the nutrients that they have consumed. If animals are improperly fed and not provided with the right nutrients, eating them does not benefit us, it actually harms us. If chickens are fed chemicals, and we eat chickens, we are essentially eating those same chemicals.

Humans do not need to eat meat. Our body is actually structured to only consume fruits, vegetables, seeds, nuts and grains. We do not have

---

[25] http://ageconsearch.umn.edu/bitstream/28675/1/sp03-02.pdf

[26] http://www.foodcircles.missouri.edu/07contable.pdf

[27] http://www.100daysofrealfood.com/2010/04/28/some-highlights-from-the-food-inc-documentary/

carnivorous teeth, capable of chewing raw meat. We have flat teeth, with a small mouth opening, contrary to that of carnivores. We do not have a short intestinal track capable of quick digestion, we have a long intestinal track that is 10 to 12 times the length of our body.[28] The reason we have eaten meat for generations was for survival, when the nutrients we needed were not readily available, so we were forced to obtain them through animals.

"A human body in no way resembles those that were born for ravenousness; it hath no hawk's bill, no sharp talon, no roughness of teeth, no such strength of stomach or heat of digestion, as can be sufficient to convert or alter such heavy and fleshy fare. But if you will contend that you were born to an inclination to such food as you have now a mind to eat, do you then yourself kill what you would eat. But do it yourself, without the help of a chopping-knife, mallet or axe, as wolves, bears, and lions do, who kill and eat at once. Rend an ox with thy teeth, worry a hog with thy mouth, tear a lamb or a hare in pieces, and fall on and eat it alive as they do. But if thou had rather stay until what thou eat is to become dead, and if thou art loath to force a soul out of its body, why then dost thou against nature eat an animate thing? There is nobody that is willing to eat even a lifeless and a dead thing even as it is; so they boil it, and roast it, and alter it by fire and medicines, as it were, changing and quenching the slaughtered gore with thousands of sweet sauces, that the palate being thereby deceived may admit of such uncouth fare."

— Plutarch

Since the agricultural revolution, when humans learned to produce mass amounts of food, the consumption of meat has been unnecessary. What sense does it make to kill an animal because you enjoy the way it tastes? It might be easy to ignore the issue when you don't see it first hand, but billions of animals are killed for meat every day, living their brief lives

---

[28] http://www.celestialhealing.net/physicalveg3.htm

tortured in a slaughterhouse. We kill animals for profit and pleasure, when we have the resources to get the nutrients we need from plants that we can produce ourselves.

The billions of chickens, turkeys, pigs and cows who are raised for food each year in the U.S. produce a tremendous amount of excrement, releasing methane and other greenhouse gases into our atmosphere. Methane, which is at least 20 times more potent than carbon dioxide, accounts for 10% of the greenhouse-gas emissions in the U.S.[29] The 523 million chickens raised and killed each year in Delaware and Maryland alone generate enough waste to fill the dome of the U.S. Capitol about 50 times in a single year, or almost once a week. And each cow emits approximately 66 to 79 gallons of methane every single day.[30] There are currently 88 million cattle in the United States. That's between five billion, eight hundred eight million (5,808,000,000) and six billion, nine hundred fifty-two million (6,952,000,000) gallons of methane per day. Together, these cows reportedly produce more methane than landfills, natural gas leaks, and fracking combined.[31]

A German study conducted in 2008 concluded that a meat-eater's diet is responsible for more than seven times the volume of greenhouse-gas emissions than a vegan's diet.

---

[29] http://www3.epa.gov/climatechange/ghgemissions/gases/ch4.html

[30] http://www.collective-evolution.com/2015/06/02/distrubing-aerial-photos-show-what-killing-billions-of-animals-for-meat-is-doing-to-the-environment/comment-page-1/

[31] http://www.cowspiracy.com/facts/

A Loma Linda University study shows that vegans have the smallest carbon footprint, generating a 41.7% smaller volume of greenhouse gasses than meat-eaters do, and a 13.9% smaller volume than vegetarians.[32]

The president of the Worldwatch Institute has said that the "world's supersized appetite for meat" is one of the main reasons why greenhouse-gas emissions are increasing rapidly.[33]

According to researchers from the University of California-Riverside, cooking just one charbroiled burger causes as much pollution as driving an 18-wheeler for 143 miles.[34] Researchers at the University of Chicago concluded that switching from a standard American diet to vegan meals is more effective in the fight against climate change than switching from a standard American car to a hybrid.[35]

It is no secret that in Nature animals eat other animals to survive, but our survival is not dependent on meat anymore. We have discovered many more effective ways to sustain our health. It is understandable if meat needs to be eaten out of necessity, but we need to realize each act for what it is. There is a huge difference between one person killing an animal to feed themselves and their family, and having thousands of established slaughterhouses that require massive amounts of resources to maintain, just so that they can torture and kill animal life for profit and pleasure. Each time you buy meat, you are supporting an industry that is involved in the tragic process of killing

---

[32] http://www.huffingtonpost.com/tracy-reiman/electric-cars-arent-enoug_b_5187669.html

[33] http://www.worldwatch.org/global-meat-production-and-consumption-continue-rise-1

[34] http://losangeles.cbslocal.com/2012/09/18/study-air-pollution-from-burger-joints-worse-than-trucks/

[35] http://www-news.uchicago.edu/releases/06/060413.diet.shtml

and butchering millions of animals, polluting the environment, and destroying the health of both the planet and the human species.

Take into consideration the effect that a meat-eater's diet has on the world. Billions of animals are tortured and slaughtered for profit, each of which produce a considerable amount of waste which is harmful to our planet, simply because people enjoy the way that they taste. We do not need to eat meat; we are perfectly capable of surviving, and even thriving, without it, yet most people eat it with every meal. The majority of meat-eaters are unaware that they are contributing to the meat industry, increasing the practice of slaughtering animals. Most meat-eaters are also unaware of how these animals are treated prior to ending up on their plates. If we had to individually kill each animal we ate, I think that we would all have a different perspective on the meat industry and its practices.

> "A man can live and be healthy without killing animals for food; therefore, if he eats meat, he participates in taking animal life merely for the sake of his appetite."
>
> – *Leo Tolstoy*

A 2009 Worldwatch report states that livestock is responsible for 51% of all global greenhouse gas emissions, with over 116,000 pounds of animal excrement produced every second in the United States alone.[36]

Our current system of food production simply does not make sense. More than a third of the world's grain is fed to livestock, which return to us only a fraction of those nutrients. A large amount of land is needed to

---

[36] http://www.worldwatch.org/node/6294

produce the grains needed to feed the livestock, and this land is often obtained by burning down rainforests and other ecosystem-dense land.

Overfishing is also a tragic issue with our agricultural system. Billions of fish are taken out of the ocean every year and are not able to reproduce as fast as they are being fished. Fishing nets also catch more than intended, including many animals like turtles, dolphins, sharks, and sea birds.[37] As a result of overfishing, our oceans are dying and the intricate web of marine life has been permanently affected.

The modern agricultural industry and its practices are not sustainable. An acre of rainforest is cleared every second, and the majority of this land is used to provide land for animal agriculture.[38] Rather than growing food to feed to all of the Earth's people, we grow food to feed the animals that feed the people of more industrialized nations such as the United States, Canada, United Kingdom, and Europe, while leaving billions to starve and live in poverty.

The modern agricultural industry is the biggest contributor to soil pollution, air pollution, water pollution, habitat loss, species extinction, and of course human illness. Most of the meat produced is heavily processed and treated with chemicals, which are terrible for our health.

The U.S. Food and Drug Administration (FDA) has admitted that chicken meat sold in the USA contains arsenic, a cancer-causing toxic chemical that is fatal in high doses. Arsenic has been added to the chicken feed, where it ends up in the chicken meat to be consumed by humans. So for the last sixty years,

---

[37] http://wwf.panda.org/what_we_do/endangered_species/cetaceans/threats/bycatch/
[38] http://www.scientificamerican.com/article/earth-talks-daily-destruction/

American consumers who eat conventional chicken have been swallowing arsenic, a known cancer-causing chemical.

The term "you are what you eat" should be taken more literally. Every 35 days your skin replaces itself, your liver replaces itself in about 6 weeks, your bones replace themselves in about 3 months, and the entire human body is replaced approximately every 7 years. Your body makes these new cells from the food that you eat. What you eat literally becomes you. If the food you eat is unhealthy and contains chemicals, you will become unhealthy in return. Most diseases, including cancer and diabetes, can be traced back to a person's diet.[39]

---

[39] http://www.feelguide.com/2010/11/13/did-you-know-the-regeneration-of-the-human-body-2/

Chapter 7. Pesticides

Not only is the meat that we consume contaminated, but most vegetables, fruits and grains are contaminated as well. Pesticides are used to grow a majority of the food we eat. They stay on our food after we wash them, they stay in our bodies for years after we eat them, and they impact our environment every time we use them.

In 2007, a systematic review found that "most studies on non-Hodgkins lymphoma and leukemia showed positive associations with pesticide exposure" and concluded that cosmetic use of pesticides should be decreased.[40] Strong evidence also exists for other negative outcomes from pesticide exposure, including neurological deficiencies, birth defects, fetal death, and neurodevelopmental disorder.

According to The Stockholm Convention on Persistent Organic Pollutants, 9 of the 12 most dangerous and persistent chemicals are pesticides used in our food.[41]

These chemicals are not only harmful to our bodies but they are harmful to our environment. Runoff can carry pesticides into aquatic environments while wind can carry them to other fields, grazing areas, human settlements and undeveloped areas, potentially affecting other species.

The purpose of pesticides is to eliminate insects and other pests from damaging crops, in order to ensure that there will be enough produced to

---

[40] http://www.ncbi.nlm.nih.gov/pubmed/17934034

[41] http://www.pops.int/documents/guidance/beg_guide.pdf

keep up with the demand. The problem with pesticides is that they do not always work, and after a few generations, the pests usually become immune through the process of natural selection.

The more a pesticide is used, the greater the chance that the insects targeted will develop immunity to the chemical. Pesticide resistance is not only very common, but it also usually happens rather quickly. Sometimes all it takes is a single generation. Imagine that a group of insects survives the pesticide and is able to reproduce. More likely than not, the offspring will be resistant to the pesticide from birth. Those that are not immune will die, while the strongest will survive. Since many insects reproduce quickly, several generations can be born within months or even weeks. By the time a few generations have passed, all insects are likely to be resistant to the pesticide. This has resulted in stronger pesticides, and new ways of producing pesticides.

Bayer CropScience, a division of Bayer AG (the pharmaceutical company that makes Bayer aspirin), developed a class of pesticides called systemic pesticides.[42] Systemic pesticides are taken up inside the plant, typically through the root system, so that every part of the plant then contains the chemical. The chemical is soluble enough in water that it can be absorbed by a plant and moved around in its tissues.

When chemicals that are designed to kill are introduced into delicately balanced ecosystems, they can set damage in motion that reverberates through the food web for years.

Five great extinction events have reshaped Earth in the past 439 million years, each wiping out between half and 95% of planetary life. The most

---

[42] http://www.honeycolony.com/article/setting-the-record-straight-on-bayer-cropscience/

recent was the killing off of dinosaurs. Today, we're living through a sixth great cataclysm. Seven in ten biologists believe that mass extinction poses an even greater threat to humanity than the global warming which contributes to it.[43]

Species extinction is primarily driven by the loss of habitat, pollution of ecosystems, exposure to toxic chemicals, and the death of animals that are a primary food source. These dominant causes of species extinction are all primarily triggered by modern agriculture. If we do not change the way that we produce and distribute our food, we will continue to do damage to the planet and all of the life that inhabits it.

Amphibians were some of the first species to start dying off from exposure to toxic chemicals. In 1998, scientists identified the cause as a type of fungus, with population declines showing a strong correlation to pesticide exposure.[44] A primary herbicide manufacturer, Syngenta, created an herbicide they call "Aatrex," more commonly known as atrazine. More than 75 million pounds of the herbicide is used on U.S. farms every year, making it the second most-used pesticide in agriculture. It contaminates water supplies throughout the Midwest at levels above those found to turn male tadpoles into female frogs in the lab.[45]

In the 1990s, the Syngenta Corporation funded Dr. Tyrone Hayes of the University of California, Berkeley to study the environmental impacts of atrazine. When Dr. Hayes discovered ovaries growing in the testes of male frogs raised in atrazine-contaminated water, Syngenta refused to let him publish his findings.

---

[43] http://www.panna.org/resources/environmental-impacts

[44] http://e360.yale.edu/feature/behind_mass_die_offs_pesticides_lurk_as_culprit/2228/

[45] http://news.berkeley.edu/2015/01/23/new-documentary-tells-biologist-tyrone-hayes-tale-of-atrazine-frogs-and-syngenta/

Hayes repeated the experiment with independent funding, and today continues research on atrazine's dramatic impacts on amphibians.

Atrazine's effect on amphibians is shocking: 10% of male frogs raised in atrazine-laced water developed into females. Genetically, the frogs are still males, but morphologically they are completely female—they can even mate successfully with other males and lay viable eggs.[46]

The next animal to die off was honey bees. Bee populations have dropped by 29%-36% each year since 2006.[47] The reason is due to the pesticides we use on plants. Bees pollinate plants and without them much of the food we eat could not be produced. Pollination occurs when pollen is transferred from the anther (male part) of the plant, to the stigma (female part) of the plant, thereby enabling fertilization and reproduction.

Bees pollinate flowers allowing them to produce fruits and vegetables. One third of the food we eat depends on bees for pollination. So when the insects suddenly started dying off and abandoning their hives in 2006, scientists, beekeepers and farmers sounded the alarm. Researchers called the phenomenon "Colony Collapse Disorder," and found the cause was a direct link to pesticides. Most insecticides are inherently toxic to bees, and a recent study found a cocktail of toxic pesticides in the wax and honey of commercial hives.[48]

"If the bee disappeared off the surface of the globe, then man would have only four years of life left. No more bees, no more pollination, no more plants, no more animals, no more man."

– Albert Einstein

---

[46] http://www.amphibians.org/wp-content/uploads/2013/07/1-TAW-intro.pdf

[47] http://phys.org/news/2010-03-scientists-stumped-bee-population-declines.html

[48] http://www.honeycolony.com/article/setting-the-record-straight-on-bayer-cropscience/

The most recent victims to suffer from pesticide exposure are bats.[49] In 2006, the first cave floors were found covered with dead bats in the Northeast. Some scientists believe that, like amphibians, bats have become more susceptible to deadly disease (in this case, White Nose Syndrome) because pesticides weaken their immune systems. A growing body of evidence points towards pesticide exposure – even at so-called "safe levels" – as a key contributor to these and other problems for wildlife.

The increasing potency of pesticides has affected the entire animal kingdom. Insects consume the pesticides and carry them inside of their bodies before slowly being killed by the poison. Animals eating these contaminated insects become infected from the poison as well. Our food is toxic due to the use of powerful pesticides.

When chemical pesticides and fertilizers were first introduced to the farming community they were accepted without much consideration of their effect on the environment. Farmers only noticed that pests were taken care of and their crops grew faster. Most people failed to recognize that the pesticides were polluting the soil and killing the animals that help maintain the natural balance of the ecosystem.

Now after years of using these chemicals, farmers have damaged their land and are now dependent upon pesticides and fertilizers to produce their crops. Although people are beginning to recognize the damage that

---

[49] http://www.batconservation.org/about-bats/conservation/white-nose-syndrome?gclid=Cj0KEQjwmNuuBRDTu5rDjr2kxJsBEiQAWlm6UsXm1YYEzZqXXHX-QbzFhb1GINAI9waubl34HOxv6x4aApzu8P8HAQ

chemical pesticides and fertilizers do to crops, and farmers are shifting toward more natural methods of farming.

This shift from conventional agriculture to natural farming is difficult for the farmer to achieve, because chemically grown produce is in high demand. People fail to recognize the farmer-consumer relationship. When consumers prefer to purchase conventionally grown produce, the farmer has to keep up with the demands or suffer losing money.

In nature, fruits and vegetables rarely grow to resemble the conventionally grown produce. Conventional farmers use chemical fertilizers to grow larger fruits, then when the products are shipped they are covered in a protective wax to prevent bruising. People judge produce by the appearance, picking out the biggest and most colorful fruits and vegetables.

Nature does not yield perfect looking produce; usually, fruits and vegetables are lumpy, bruised, or oddly shaped. Since people prefer to buy the chemically made produce based off of its appearance, they create a larger market for these products and the farmer is forced to produce his crops this way to meet the market demands.

If natural farming is not practiced, natural food will not be available to the public. But if a natural diet is not established, the farmer will remain confused about what to grow. Unless people become natural people, natural farming will not be practiced and natural food will not be available.

The use of pesticides is a pervasive problem with modern agriculture, affecting the food that we eat, the health of our bodies, and the health of the environment overall. However, perhaps an even bigger threat to the health of humanity is genetically modified organisms.

Chapter 8. Genetically Modified Organisms

A genetically modified organism (GMO) is an organism whose genetic material has been altered using genetic engineering techniques.[50] Although labeling of GMO products in the marketplace is required in 64 countries, it is not required in the United States, and the U.S. FDA recognizes no distinction between marketed GMO and non-GMO foods.[51]

The American Academy of Environmental Medicine (AAEM) has done animal studies showing the consumption of GMO foods is related to organ damage, gastrointestinal and immune system disorders, accelerated aging, and infertility.[52] Human studies show how genetically modified (GM) food can leave material behind inside us, possibly causing long-term problems. Genes inserted into GM soy, for example, can transfer into the DNA of bacteria living inside us, and the toxic insecticide produced by GM corn was found in the blood of pregnant women and their unborn fetuses.[53]

Numerous health problems increased after GMOs were introduced in 1996. The percentage of Americans with three or more chronic illnesses jumped from 7% to 13% in just 9 years; food allergies skyrocketed, and disorders such as autism, reproductive disorders, digestive problems, and others are on the rise. By mixing genes from totally unrelated species,

---

[50] http://www.livescience.com/40895-gmo-facts.html

[51] http://www.responsibletechnology.org/gmo-education

[52] http://responsibletechnology.org/gmo-education/health-risks/

[53] http://responsibletechnology.org/10-reasons-to-avoid-gmos/

genetic engineering unleashes a host of unpredictable side effects.[54] Moreover, irrespective of the type of genes that are inserted, the very process of creating a GM plant can result in massive collateral damage that produces new toxins, allergens, carcinogens, and nutritional deficiencies.

GMOs cross-pollinate and their seeds can travel. It is impossible to fully clean up our contaminated gene pool. Self-propagating GMO pollution will outlast the effects of global warming and nuclear waste. The potential impact is huge, threatening the health of future generations. GMO contamination has also caused economic losses for organic and non-GMO farmers who often struggle to keep their crops pure. GM crops and their associated herbicides can harm birds, insects, amphibians, marine ecosystems, and soil organisms. They reduce bio-diversity, pollute water resources, and are unsustainable. For example, GM crops are eliminating habitat for monarch butterflies, whose populations are down 50% in the U.S.[55]

The argument behind genetically modified foods is that it will help support the demand for food in an increasing world population, even though GMOs do not, on average, increase yields at all. This was evident in the Union of Concerned Scientists' 2009 report "Failure to Yield"—the definitive study to date on GM crops and yield.[56]

The International Assessment of Agricultural Knowledge, Science and Technology for Development (IAASTD) report, authored by more than 400 scientists and backed by 58 governments, stated that GM crop yields were

[54] http://foodshedalliance.org/2014/05/25/the-case-for-labeling-genetically-modified-food/

[55] http://www.nongmoproject.org/learn-more/

[56] http://www.ucsusa.org/sites/default/files/legacy/assets/documents/food_and_agriculture/failure-to-yield.pdf

"highly variable" and in some cases, "yields declined." The report noted, "Assessment of the technology lags behind its development, information is anecdotal and contradictory, and uncertainty about possible benefits and damage is unavoidable." They determined that the current GMOs have nothing to offer the goals of reducing hunger and poverty, improving nutrition, health and rural livelihoods, and facilitating social and environmental sustainability. The funding of GMOs diverts money and resources that would otherwise be spent on more safe, reliable, and appropriate technologies.

In the U.S., GMOs are in as much as 80% of conventional processed food. Most processed food is a by-product of corn or soy. The majority of both corn and soy produced in the U.S. is genetically modified. As a result, the majority of our food supply consists of GMOs.[57] Genetically modified foods have many negative health effects and no one knows what the long-term effects will be.[58]

According to the United States FDA, its responsibilities include "protecting the public health by assuring that foods are safe, wholesome, sanitary and properly labeled." This responsibility entails regulating a large number of companies producing this nation's food, making appointments to the high-level positions within the agency very important.

Most high-level FDA employees have a background in either medicine or law, but one of the largest private-sector sources is the Monsanto Company.[59] Monsanto is the biggest agricultural biotech company, and the leading producer of GMOs. Over the past couple of decades, at least seven

---

[57] http://phys.org/news/2013-06-gmo-corn-soybeans-dominate.html

[58] http://www.collective-evolution.com/2014/04/08/10-scientific-studies-proving-gmos-can-be-harmful-to-human-health/

[59] http://rense.com/general33/fd.htm

high-ranking employees in the FDA have an employment history with the Monsanto Company.[60] Figure 8-1, from Geke.us, shows the many connections between Monsanto and the U.S. Government:

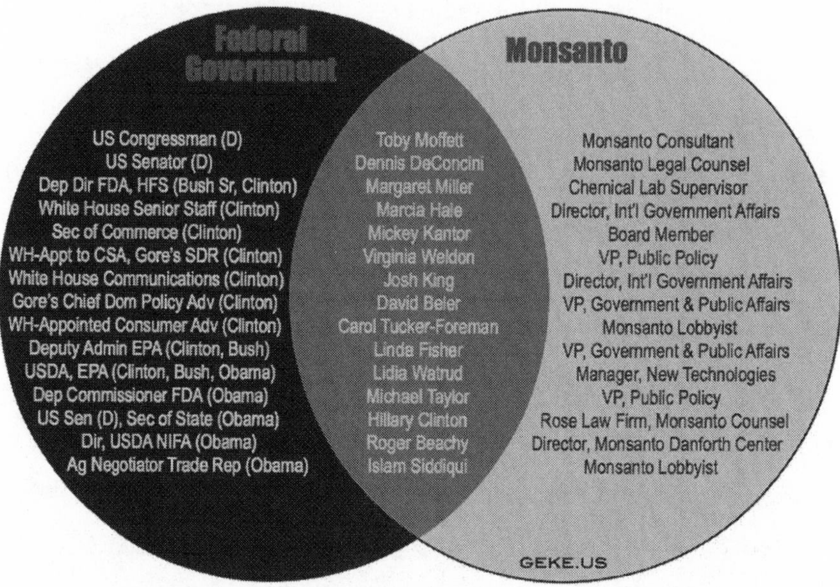

Figure 8-1. Monsanto's Ties to the U.S. Government[61]

By avoiding GMOs, you contribute to the coming tipping point of consumer rejection, forcing them out of our food supply. Because GMOs give no consumer benefits, if even a small percentage of us start rejecting brands that contain them, GM ingredients will become a marketing liability. Food companies will kick them out. In Europe, for example, the tipping point was achieved in 1999, just after a high-profile GMO safety scandal hit the papers and alerted citizens to the potential dangers.

---

[60] http://readersupportednews.org/news-section2/318-66/10006-monsanto-employees-in-the-halls-of-government

[61] Geke.us

In the US, a consumer rebellion against GM bovine growth hormone has also reached a tipping point, and kicked the cow drug out of dairy products produced by Wal-Mart, Starbucks, Dannon, Yoplait, and most of America's dairies. We can prevent the use of GMOs by alerting the public of their health effects and refusing to purchase their products.

To identify which fruits and vegetables contain GMOs or pesticides, look at the labeled stickers that are placed on them (fig. 8-2). The labels have numbers located above the barcode. Labels with 4 digits (usually beginning with a 4) are conventionally grown and contain pesticides.

Figure 8-2. Identifying Organic, Conventional, and GMO Foods by Their Labels[62]

Example: 4139. Labels with 5 digits that start with an 8 are genetically modified. Example: 84805. Labels with 5 digits that begin with a 9 are organic, and are the only ones that you should purchase. Example: 94129. By paying attention to the food you buy, you can support your health and

---

[62] http://fittipdaily.com/what-do-the-stickers-on-your-produce-really-mean-13770/

stop supporting the companies that are damaging your health and the environment through their practices of food production.

To avoid the negative health effects linked to certain foods, stop eating junk food, start buying products that are organic with no GMOs or pesticides, and start eating a healthier diet.

The ideal human diet is a whole food plant-based diet. Consume plant-based foods in forms as close to their natural state as possible. Over 80% of your meals should be raw. Cooking food kills the enzymes that are needed for your body to absorb nutrients. Eat a variety of vegetables, fruits, raw nuts and seeds, beans and legumes, and pseudo-grains. Avoid heavily processed foods and animal products. Stay away from added salt, oil, and sugar. Aim to get 80 percent of your calories from carbohydrates, 10 percent from fat, and 10 percent from protein. By following this diet, you will have a huge beneficial impact on your health. Believe it or not, most diseases are linked to poor nutrition.

"People are fed by the food industry, which pays no attention to health, and are treated by the health industry, which pays no attention to food."
– Wendell Berry

Chapter 9. The Medical Industry

The pharmaceutical drug industry is a half-trillion dollar per year global industry, with almost 300 billion dollars in the United States alone.[63] The pharmaceutical companies and their shareholders rely on people to be sick, or else their stocks will plummet. There is no money to be made in health.[64]

The mainstream medical journals publish articles that support the pharmaceutical industry, and while there are thousands of articles that suggest nutrition is the key factor to good health, none of them are published by the mainstream medical journals.

Doctors are not trained to know about nutrition; they are trained to prescribe drugs that will treat the symptoms of illness, rather than treating the root cause of the illness. Less than 6% of graduating physicians in the US receive any formal training in nutrition.[65] Each year 106,000 people die from pharmaceutical drugs, not including overdoses; these people died from the side effects of taking these drugs as directed.[66] People who work for the pharmaceutical companies test the drugs. The people that regulate the drugs should not work for the same people that make them.

---

[63] http://www.phrma.org/sites/default/files/pdf/2015_phrma_profile.pdf

[64] http://www.forbes.com/sites/johnlamattina/2014/07/29/do-drug-companies-make-drugs-or-money/

[65] http://doctorwatch.blogspot.com/2010/06/ray-dstrand-md-warns-you-of-danger-you.html

[66] http://www.huffingtonpost.com/rabbi-shmuly-yanklowitz/pharmaceutical-drug-_b_4067827.html

When you supply yourself with the proper vitamins and minerals, you enable the body to heal itself. Hippocrates, the father of modern medicine, believed that food was the best medicine, and that the body has its own natural healing mechanism.

"The natural healing force within each of us is the greatest force in getting well."
– Hippocrates

The human body possesses an enormous, astonishing, and persistent capacity to heal itself. Disease generally occurs when we abuse our bodies or deprive them of basic requirements to keep us healthy over extended periods. If we are constantly putting food in our bodies that is not nutritious, while also not consuming any nutritious foods, we will develop disease and illness in our body. When we supply our bodies with the proper nutrients, they will not develop disease in the first place.

"Let food be thy medicine and medicine be thy food."
– Hippocrates

Chapter 10. Nutrition

When we eat food, some components of food are broken down into sugar for energy. Our bodies use the sugar to make the energy we need to move and grow. Energy allows all of our organs to function, allows us to move, talk, run, think, breathe and do all of the things we do every moment. Food for humans is like electricity for a computer. Without electricity, a computer cannot do anything. Without food, our bodies cannot do anything.[67]

We cannot gain our energy directly from the Sun, so we have to eat plants that gather their energy from the Sun through photosynthesis.[68] [69] Animals also gain their energy from plants, so we can also gather energy by eating animals, but it is less efficient since the nutrients have already been previously processed. When we eat a plant or animal, we obtain the energy that that organism contained. If we eat plants that were deprived of nutrients and supplemented with chemicals for growth, we take on the energy of that plant once it is consumed. Similarly, if we eat a cow that was fed chemically grown grains, then raised in a negative and harmful environment (slaughterhouse), we take on the energy of that animal once it is consumed by us. That is why it is critical to understand where your food comes from, how it was grown, what it contains, and how it will affect your health.

One thing that most people do not understand when it comes to health is the balance between an alkaline and acidic environment within our bodies.

---

[67] http://www.ftexploring.com/me/me2.html
[68] http://scienceline.ucsb.edu/getkey.php?key=4062
[69] http://biology.clc.uc.edu/courses/bio104/photosyn.htm

The balance of acid and alkaline within the body is referred to as pH (meaning "potential of hydrogen"), and is measured on a scale ranging from pH 1 (most acidic) to pH 14 (most alkaline). A neutral or good pH balance is 7.35; maintaining this balance is critical for good health. If the body's pH drops, meaning it becomes too acidic; the likelihood of developing illnesses rises severely. An acidic environment within the body negatively affects your health at the cellular level.[70] It is impossible for the body to be in a state of good health if it is too acidic. We need to eat more alkaline forming foods to balance the pH level within our bodies. Interestingly, it is not possible for cancer to form in an alkaline environment; demonstrating the importance of alkalinity in disease prevention.

Basically all fruits and vegetables are highly alkaline forming, as are most pseudo-grains. Pseudo-grains are a gluten-free alternative to grains. Grains are actually harmful to the body and include many toxic anti-nutrients and inflammatory proteins like gluten. Examples of pseudo-grains are quinoa, buckwheat, and amaranth. Beans and grains are typically neutral or slightly acid forming, along with most herbs. The foods that are highly acid forming are coincidentally foods that are most common in the North American diet. These foods include: commercial breakfast cereals, pasta, refined wheat flour, white rice, beef, pork, poultry, shellfish, butter, cheese, cream, milk, artificial sweeteners, white sugar, candy, coffee, peanuts, prescription drugs, soft drinks, soy protein isolate, and whey protein isolate. While most people do eat alkaline forming foods, it is hardly enough to balance the acidity formed by the base of their diet. By focusing

---

[70] http://healthwyze.org/index.php/component/content/article/361-the-relationship-between-body-ph-and-disease-and-other-facts-youre-not-supposed-to-know.html

on the pH balance within our bodies we can greatly improve our level of health and overall wellness.[71]

There is no diet that is right for everybody; every individual is different and requires a diet that is relevant to their lifestyle and their body's needs. Though it is important to familiarize yourself with the various nutrients that our bodies require for optimal health, understanding why they matter, and what foods they are most plentiful in so that we can include these foods in our diets, thus improving the quality of our life experience.

According to the U.S. National Library of Medicine, "Vitamins are a group of substances that are needed for normal cell function, growth, and development."[72]

Vitamin A helps the body resist infection and allows the body to use its reserves for repairing and regenerating muscle tissue. Vitamin A helps support growth and repair of muscle and maintains red and white blood cells. Best sources of Vitamin A: orange and dark green vegetables, including pumpkin, carrots, squash, sweet potatoes, broccoli, kale, parsley and spinach; apricots, mango, papaya, and cantaloupe.

Vitamin B1 helps the body convert carbohydrates into energy. Maintaining high energy levels depends in part on maintaining adequate B1 in the diet. Best sources of Vitamin B1: legumes, nuts, brown rice, nutritional yeast, and pseudo-grains.

Vitamin B2 helps break down amino acids (protein) for the body to use. Like B1, B2 helps convert carbohydrates into energy. It also contributes to healthy red blood cell production. Best sources of Vitamin B2: legumes, nuts, brown rice, nutritional yeast, and pseudo-grains.

Vitamin B3 is essential for the body's breakdown and utilization of carbohydrate and protein. As with other B vitamins, vitamin B3 plays an integral part in the conversion of food into energy. It also plays a key role in keeping the digestive system healthy, allowing the body to get more

---

[71] http://www.webmd.com/diet/alkaline-diets

[72] https://www.nlm.nih.gov/medlineplus/ency/article/002399.htm

out of the food it consumes. Best sources of vitamin B3: beets, sunflower seeds, and nutritional yeast.

Vitamin B5, as well as all B vitamins, helps convert food into energy. It also facilitates the production of steroids – an integral part of the regeneration process after physical exertion. Best Sources of Vitamin B5: seeds, pseudo-grains, avocados.

Vitamin B6 aids in the production of antibodies—essential for warding off infection and maintaining the ability to recover from exertion quickly. Vitamin B6 also contributes to cardiovascular health, helping the heart efficiently circulate blood in a greater volume. Best sources of Vitamin B6: pseudo-grains, bananas, brown rice, walnuts, avocados, and oats.

Vitamin B12 is essential for a healthy nervous system, aiding in coordination and smooth muscle movement. As with other B vitamins, B12 plays a role in production of red blood cells and conversion of food into energy. Unlike other B vitamins, Vitamin B12 is not plentiful in most foods. Vitamin B12 is a very important nutrient. In our modern food supply, B12 is found mostly in animal products. The bacteria in the stomach of vegetarian animals such as cows (and also goats, sheep, deer, etc.) can synthesize B12, which is then absorbed by their small intestines, thereby imparting B12 into the animal. So non-vegetarians get their B12 from eating these animal products. Humans also make B12-synthesizing bacteria in their large intestine. The challenge lies in the fact that it's actually absorbed in the small intestine, which is upstream. Fortunately, the cells of our stomach actually make something called "intrinsic factor" which seeks out B12 from food and together they make their way to the small intestine where the B12 can be absorbed. So we need this intrinsic factor because B12 is the only nutrient that requires help in order to be absorbed. In the past, B12 was plentiful because we ate foods that were not as deep cleaned and practically sanitized as they are today, so the bacteria in our guts were able to synthesize the B12 we needed. Since times have changed, it is recommended that both vegans and meat-eaters supplement their diet with B12. The best sources of Vitamin B12: Vitamin B12 supplements, AFA Blue Green Algae, Chlorella, and nutritional yeast.

Vitamin C is a powerful antioxidant and plays a major role in reducing damage to body tissue and muscle caused by physical activity. Cellular damage that occurs as a result of environmental factors such as pollution will also be minimized by frequent ingestion of Vitamin C. Best sources of Vitamin C: most fruits and vegetables (especially citrus fruits).

Vitamin D allows the body to absorb calcium more efficiently. Best sources of Vitamin D: exposure to sunlight, nutritional yeast.

Vitamin E, like Vitamin C, is a powerful antioxidant. Vitamin E promotes cardiovascular health, proper growth hormone production, and muscle rejuvenation. Best sources of Vitamin E: flaxseed oil, hemp oil, pumpkin seed oil, raspberry seed oil, cranberry seed oil, pomegranate seed oil, nuts, and avocados.

Vitamin K provides the heart with the nutrients it needs for optimal function. It also plays a significant role in blood clotting. Best sources of Vitamin K: leafy green vegetables, pine nuts.

Calcium repairs and strengthens your bones, plays a major role in muscle contraction, and ensures a rhythmic heartbeat. Best sources of calcium: leafy green vegetables, sesame seeds, almond milk.

Chromium works with other vitamins and minerals to turn carbohydrate into usable energy. Best sources of Chromium: pseudo-grains, nuts, nutritional yeast, black pepper, and thyme.

Copper assists iron absorption in the body. With iron, copper plays a role in the transport of oxygen throughout the body. Copper also works in concert with antioxidants to reduce effects of environmental and physical damage, providing the body with a strong platform to regenerate and build strength. Best sources of copper: legumes, seeds, pseudo-grains, raisins, nuts.

Folate is a B vitamin that is found naturally in foods; when in supplement form it is called folic acid. Folate works in tandem with Vitamin B12 to help produce oxygen-carrying red blood cells. Folate plays an integral role in helping the body make use of dietary protein, facilitating muscle repair. The heart relies on Folate, in part, to maintain a smooth, rhythmic beat and a higher tolerance for physical activity. Best sources of Folate: leafy green vegetables, legumes, pseudo-grains, orange juice, nutritional yeast.

Iodine is integral to thyroid hormone production. Thyroid hormone assists the cells in the fabrication of protein and the metabolism of fats. Best sources of iodine: sea vegetables, strawberries.

Iron fabricates hemoglobin to facilitate red blood cell health. A well maintained iron level ensures the body is able to deliver oxygen-rich blood to the hard working extremities, maximizing efficacy. Best sources of iron: spinach, legumes, and pumpkin seeds.

Magnesium is critical for muscle function; it helps the heart beat rhythmically by allowing it to relax between beats, allowing all other muscles to relax. Magnesium also assists in calcium's bone production. Best sources of Magnesium: leafy green vegetables, string beans, legumes, pseudo-grains, bananas, nuts, avocados.

Manganese contributes to an accelerated process of recovery, essential for those who are physically active. It is also a cofactor in energy production, metabolizing proteins and fats. Best sources of manganese: leafy green vegetables, legumes, pseudo-grains, nuts, brown rice.

Molybdenum, a trace mineral, moves stored iron from the liver into the bloodstream, aids in the detoxification process and helps the body rid itself of potentially toxic material, minimizing stress. Best sources of molybdenum: legumes, pseudo-grains, nuts.

Phosphorus allows the body to use food as fuel. It works with calcium in the production, repair, and maintenance of bones. Best sources of phosphorus: pseudo-grains, most tropical fruit.

Potassium, an electrolyte, helps the body maintain fluid balance and therefore hydration. Smooth muscle contractions, nerve impulse transmission, and cell integrity are also greatly affected by potassium intake. Best sources of potassium: leafy green vegetables, most fruits (especially bananas and kiwis).

Selenium preserves muscle tissue elasticity, allowing fluent, supple, movement. A trace mineral, selenium combines with other antioxidants to shield red blood cells from damage done by physical exertion. It also improves immune function. Best sources of selenium: Brazil nuts, walnuts, brown rice, and nutritional yeast.

Zinc allows the body to use dietary protein as building blocks for the regeneration of muscles. Zinc also plays a major role in proper immune function. Best sources of zinc: pseudo-grains, pumpkin seeds, and nutritional yeast.

Carbohydrate is abundant, present in most foods, and for non-active people, a regular diet will supply the body with all the carbohydrate it needs. However, active people must increase the amount of carbohydrate in their diet to maintain energy levels and replenish muscles post-exertion. Carbohydrates also assist in the digestion and utilization of all other foods. Carbohydrates are made up of three components: sugar, starch, and fiber. When grains are refined, the fiber is removed, increasing the percentage of starch and sugar. Refined carbohydrates are most common in white bread, pasta, donuts and many other foods most commonly consumed in the average North American's diet. Fiber rich carbohydrates are needed for the body to be healthy and function properly. Best sources of carbohydrates: vegetables, pseudo-grains, fruit.

Fat is the body's primary source of energy, especially when engaged in low-intensity activity. Fat ensures that fat-soluble vitamins A, D, E, and K are delivered and utilized by the body. Best sources of fat: flaxseed, hemp, pumpkin seed, nuts, coconut and avocado.

Essential Fatty Acids (EFA) are fatty acids that the body cannot produce itself, and must be ingested by eating foods rich in EFA. Omega-3 and Omega-6 are the two essential fatty acids. EFAs are important for overall health. Lending support to the healthy function of cardiovascular, immune, and nervous systems, EFAs also play a major role in promoting cell health. Best sources of Omega-3: flaxseed, chia seeds, hemp, walnuts. Best sources of Omega-6: hemp, seeds, most nuts, olive oil, avocados.

Protein assists in the fabrication of hormones, enzymes, and antibodies. Well-formed hormones are essential for a vast number of functions, primarily: muscle repair and preservation; nutrient extraction; shielding the body from bacterial and viral infection; and infusing tired muscles with more energy. Best sources of protein: leafy green vegetables, pseudo-grains, legumes, nuts and seeds (especially hemp).

It may seem difficult to get all of the above nutrients included in your diet, but as you may have noticed, there is a pattern amongst the sources of nutrients listed. Many of the sources contain nutrients from different categories. The pattern reveals that the most common foods necessary for optimal health include: leafy green vegetables, pseudo-grains, legumes, seeds, nuts, plus a variety of fruits and vegetables.[73]

I also highly recommend looking into superfoods like AFA blue-green algae, cacao, maca, marine phytoplankton, spirulina, chlorella, shilajit, and

[73] http://gentleworld.org/vegan-sources-of-vitamins-minerals/

Himalayan salt. These foods have an extremely high nutritional content and are a great addition to any diet.

Making sure that we get the nutrients that our bodies require ensures that we will be able to function at our optimal level of performance. Nutrients from food build and mend our bones, teeth, nails, skin, hair, flesh and organs and allow us to grow. We need to make sure that at least more than half of the food we consume is raw if we desire to keep our bodies in good health.[74]

Many people do not understand the importance of eating raw food. When you cook food, you kill most of the enzymes that are in it. There are living enzymes in our food that aid in digestion, and the absorption of nutrients into our body. Even lightly steaming your food will kill the majority of enzymes.

Another thing that many people are unaware of is the importance of sprouting nuts and seeds. Sprouting gives you more nutritional benefits than when an ingredient is intact in its initial state. Sprouting allows seeds to germinate, which, in turn, allows for easier digestion and absorption of nutrients. Sprouting and soaking also decreases the level of phytic acid, an enzyme inhibitor, which can block absorption of vitamins and minerals, and can cause poor digestion and disruption of healthy gut bacteria. Sprouting is easy to do, it just requires some patience, though the benefits are well worth the wait.

---

[74] http://gentleworld.org/vegan-sources-of-vitamins-minerals/

"How can you build a building that you expect to last 100 years if you put poor building materials into it? Same thing with your body, how do you expect your body to last for a long and enjoyable lifetime if you don't put the right building blocks in there?"
– Dr. Dan Rogers

Human beings require certain nutrients to maintain a healthy balance. Without properly nourishing our bodies, we cannot maintain a healthy lifestyle. Food gives us energy and nutrients to function properly. If we do not have enough energy or nutrients, the health of our body is dramatically affected, as is the health of our brain and our mood.

"To keep the body in good health is a duty... Otherwise we shall not be able to keep our mind strong and clear."
– Gautama Buddha

Good health leads to a good life experience. Our society today is extremely unhealthy, which would explain why large numbers of people are so miserable. We barely recognize this undeniable fact, even though we see the evidence on a daily basis. The reason that we are so unaware is because we have been conditioned to accept the status of our culture. We have also been fed misinformation our whole lives. History has been rewritten, corporations have taken control of our government and most major media outlets, and our educational system is flawed.

A diet that consists of food-like products rather than actual food is a diet that will dramatically affect the health of your body as well as your mind. Nutrition is a major contributor to proper cognitive functioning. Many people complain that they commonly feel a sense of sluggishness, that they lack energy or that their mind state is foggy. This state of being is a result of a nutritional imbalance and lack of exercise. The chemicals in processed food affect your cognitive functioning and the health of your body, making you feel lazy and weak. Without eating properly, you will not have enough energy for physical activity. Our technological society may distract us from the importance of exercise, but we are physical bodies living in a physical universe, and physical activity is extremely important to our health.

Chapter 11. Obesity and Physical Inactivity

Since 1980, the global obesity rate has nearly doubled, and there are now over 200 million obese men and nearly 300 million obese women, according to the Harvard School of Public Health.[75] In the United States, more than one third of adults (or 78.6 million people) are obese, according to the Centers for Disease Control and Prevention.[76]

Physical inactivity is a leading cause of death worldwide and is a major risk factor for chronic diseases such as coronary heart disease, type 2 diabetes and several different cancers.[77] In 2008, physical inactivity was responsible for an estimated five million deaths, or approximately 9 percent of the total global premature mortality.[78] In 2010, almost one-third of the world population was categorized as being physically inactive.[79] Our way of life has consisted of institutions, television screens, computers, offices, cars, buildings, and many other things that keep us blocked off from the outside world. As a result, we are out of touch with Nature, and out of touch with ourselves.

---

[75] http://www.hsph.harvard.edu/obesity-prevention-source/obesity-trends/

[76] http://www.cdc.gov/obesity/data/adult.html

[77] http://www.who.int/chp/chronic_disease_report/media/Factsheet1.pdf

[78] http://www.who.int/nmh/publications/ncd_report_chapter1.pdf

[79] http://www.fuelvm.com/acsm_eim/support_page.php?p=2

Chapter 12. Genetic Mutations

By ignoring our health and consuming unhealthy products, we are unknowingly contributing to the genetic mutation of the human species. Humans require a certain amount of nutrients from natural sources to sustain our health. When we introduce chemicals, antibiotics, pesticides, herbicides, vaccines, and other toxins into our bodies, we are altering the genetic makeup given to us by our ancestors.

According to Nature.com, Genetic mutations are changes in the genetic sequence, and they are a main cause of diversity among organisms. These changes occur at many different levels, and they can have widely differing consequences. To help put the importance of what we put in our bodies into perspective, I offer the following quote from Catherine Shanahan's book "Deep Nutrition:"

"The health of your genes represents a kind of inheritance. Two ways of thinking about this inheritance, genetic wealth and genetic momentum, help explain why some people can abuse this inheritance and, for a time, get away with it. Just as a lazy student born into a prominent family can be assured he'll get into Yale no matter his grades, healthy genes don't have to be attended to very diligently in order for their owner's bodies to look beautiful. The next generation, however, will pay the price. We've all seen the twenty-year-old supermodel who abuses her body with cigarettes and Twinkies. For years, her beautiful skeletal architecture will still shine through. Beneath the surface, poor nutrition will deprive those bones of what they need, thinning them prematurely. The connective tissue supporting her skin will begin to break down, stealing away her beauty. Most importantly, deep inside her ovaries, inside each egg, her genes will be affected. Those deleterious genetic

alterations mean that her child will have lost genetic momentum and will not have the same potential for health or beauty as she did. He or she may benefit from mom's sizable financial portfolio, but junior's genetic wealth will, unfortunately, have been drawn down. That's a real loss. Over the millennia, our genes developed under the influence of a steady stream of nourishing foods gleaned from the most nutritionally potent corners of the natural world. Today's supermodels have benefited not just from their parent's and grandparent's healthy eating habits, but from hundreds, even thousands, of generations of ancestors who, by eating the right foods, maintained -and even improved upon-the genetic heirloom that would ultimately construct a beautiful face in the womb. All of this accumulated wealth can be disposed of as easily and mindlessly as the twenty-year-old supermodel flicking away a cigarette."

– Catherine Shanahan

Our genes have been accustomed to organic material for nearly all of human history, until we began to introduce industrially made chemicals. The effects of these chemicals have already been extensively documented.

Mercury, for instance, has been linked to many diseases, including autism and Alzheimer's.[80] The United States Centers for Disease Control and Prevention (CDC) was found guilty of withholding data linking Thimerosal in vaccines to autism, non-organic sleep disorders, and speech disorders.[81] Constant exposure to small amounts of chemicals, whether they are in our food, in our air, in our water, in our cleaning materials, cars, houses, etc., as long as they are interacting with us on a daily basis, are going to severely affect our body's health and genetic makeup.

To avoid the exposure to chemicals, we must start living naturally. We are living beings on planet Earth, we are supposed to live off the planet's

[80] http://www.consumerhealth.org/articles/display.cfm?ID=20060228192435

[81] http://healthimpactnews.com/2014/cdc-caught-hiding-data-showing-mercury-in-vaccines-linked-to-autism/

natural resources, not pollute the resources that we depend on. By living a healthy lifestyle, we also stop supporting the companies that produce products that harm our health and environment.

Chapter 13. Adopting a Healthy Lifestyle

As a society and as individuals, it is important that we adopt a healthier lifestyle. The products that we buy support the companies that produce them, including their methods of production. For example, every time you buy a cheeseburger from a fast food restaurant, you support a corporation that favors animal cruelty, the poisoning of our food supply, and corporate profits over human and planetary health.

To reduce the amount of control these corporations have over our food supply, we must stop supporting them and stop purchasing their products. If everyone in the world stopped buying fast food right this moment, fast food corporations would go bankrupt within a matter of days. They would have an excessively large supply with no demand. Though this may seem like an impossible task, it is achievable through education. When the people are fully informed, there is no limit to their potential for creating positive change.

> *"I am not asking your newspapers to support the Administration, but I am asking your help in the tremendous task of informing and alerting the American people. For I have complete confidence in the response and dedication of our citizens whenever they are fully informed."*
>
> *– President John F. Kennedy*

In the next section, we will discuss why the people are currently uninformed, and why most are completely unaware of the information covered in this book.

Part II

The Enslavement of the Human Species

Chapter 14. Our Current Situation

Each day we awake to continue living out our lives. Most people head off to work to fulfill the duties of their occupation, even if it is not the occupation that they truly desire. Another majority of people go off to school, with the primary purpose of getting an education that is in line with their desired occupation.

Typically, once out of school many face the reality that the job they worked so hard to achieve was much different than they hoped it would be. Not only are they less fulfilled, but now they have an enormous amount of student loan debt to pay off, trapped in a job they don't enjoy but obligated to remain there.

Nearly everyone works, and all have different reasons why they work. Some want to improve society or their field of interest, others want money to buy material things, many do so to provide for their families. But at the root of all these reasons lies one reason that is the true reason we work: survival.

The way that our current society functions, one must work in order to gain money, which they can then use to purchase resources. We can only obtain the things we need to survive—food, water, clothing, and shelter—if we have the money to pay for it.

Logically, the question then arises, who is it that we are working for? Who is it that provides the money, who is it that controls the Earth's natural resources, and why is it that we must have money in order to access them?

We were born on this planet, so why should we have to pay in order to live on it? Surely there is more to life than servitude, but the majority of people are so preoccupied with their work and their survival that they have no time to question what they are doing, why they are doing it, and for whom they are really doing it.

Do you know whom it is that you are working for? Who the government is working for? The government is supposed to serve the people; we are not supposed to serve the government. So why have the tables turned? Why have the people become the servants rather than the ones who prosper?

The issue has many causes, but the real reason is that a handful of wealthy people have controlled our progress, and have manipulated us into accepting the progression of their agendas, rather than one that serves all of mankind.

We are the majority. It is because of us that society functions. We grow the food, we build the roads and the cars that drive on them, we maintain the land, we allow society to exist, so why do we not see the benefits of our labor? Why does it all go to these wealthy men who hide behind the logos of corporations?

It is because we allow it. We allow these people to take control of us because we have allowed them to divide us. They have divided us by race, religion, sexual orientation, and political identity—all of which are irrelevant in the grand scheme of things. They have distracted us with hundreds of small issues so that we will not focus on the real treasure that is being drained from us: our freedom.

Our freedom, our livelihood, our personal sovereignty, is governed by a handful of rich men whose greed for power and control has resulted in nearly all of the disasters we face today. All because we have allowed ourselves to conform to their authority.

They made up the laws, and we followed them. A law is only as effective as the people's belief in it. If we do not obey it, it becomes obsolete. We, the people, should determine what is right, and we as a species are all equally entitled to a fulfilled and prosperous life.

Why should a small percentage of people get to do as they please while the rest of us suffer? Why should we struggle to support their way of life while our livelihood is destroyed?

They created the money that we strive for, and we traded our freedom for their worthless pieces of paper. Money is only a tool for power and control. It keeps us living a life of servitude, and it is what allows some people to have unlimited access to the Earth's resources, while others suffer.

> *"When the last tree has been cut down, the last fish caught, the last river poisoned, only then will we realize that money cannot be eaten."*
>
> *-Native American Saying*

The people in power have manipulated us into accepting their oppression as a way of life. Though they are responsible for this corruption, we must also blame ourselves for conforming to a completely unnatural lifestyle. They only have power over us because we allow them to. We support them with every dollar we spend, every time we invest in a harmful corporation, every time we contribute to carrying out their agenda, every time we allow them to take our freedom. Without our consent they are powerless.

Through fear and manipulation, they have maintained such a powerful sense of control over us, but this control is only an illusion, and it only exists because of our ignorance. If we understand our oppressors, the history of how they gained power over us, as well as the tactics they use to maintain control, we can avoid conforming to their injustices as well as restore power back to the people.

> *"The incommensurability between the modern economic system and the people who staff it explains why modern workers have so often been depicted as 'cogs' in the larger 'machinery' of industrial civilization; for while the practical rationalization of enterprise does require workers to be consistent, predictable, precise, uniform, and even to a certain extent creative, it does not really require them to be persons, that is, to live examined lives, to grow, to develop character, to search for truth, to know themselves, etc."*
>
> *– Craig M. Gay*

The majority of people are so caught up in the rat race of modern life that they never question why they are doing what they are doing, or who they are doing it for. They just accept that this is the way life is and do whatever they can to manage, rather than trying to make it better, trying to change it, trying to improve it. They are so distracted by the stress of daily life that they are completely unaware of the forces that drive our society. They have forgotten what it means to be a real human being on planet Earth.

To understand how we have reached this point in our history, it is important to be familiar with the people who profit from humanity's hard labor. If you ask any random person why they work, they will likely reply with something like "to earn money," or "to feed my family." People work for money, but most of them don't understand the monetary system. They have no clue where money really comes from or how it dominates their lives.

Chapter 15. Money

"It is well enough that people of the nation do not understand our banking and monetary system, for if they did, I believe there would be a revolution before tomorrow morning."
– Henry Ford

Many people would say that money is the root of all evil, which is not entirely true. The root of all evil is ignorance, and the economic state of our society is a result of ignorance. Money is not evil; money is a form of exchange. It is our modern system of banking that is evil. Everybody wants money and most dedicate their lives to obtaining it. In the society that we live in, money is a necessity.

Everything has a price, even the food that we eat for our survival. It is the most common goal of the human species to acquire money; yet its origins are completely misunderstood by the general public. Do you know where money comes from? Who creates it? Who determines its value and how it affects our lives?

Most people blindly accept the fact that gaining money is essential for survival, without questioning its nature. The truth is, our current monetary system is the reason that humanity is in such a devastating state, the reason that the world is so full of corruption. Our monetary system has been limiting the potential of human beings for centuries.

Inventions that benefit humanity are hidden or destroyed because they are not profitable, or because they interfere with the business of corporations. The supreme goal of modern man is to obtain wealth, because he believes that material things will bring him happiness. He invests the majority of his time and energy into gaining money at any cost. The accumulation of wealth has contributed to man's greed and selfishness. Earning money is more important to him than being a good person, benefiting humanity, and even life itself. Modern man's sole purpose in life is gaining money. But what role does money play in our society?

Chapter 16. The Monetary System

> *"None are more hopelessly enslaved than those who falsely believe they are free."*
> *– Johann Wolfgang von Goethe*

When the U.S. government needs money, they call up the Federal Reserve Bank for, say, $1,000,000. The Fed says, "Alright, we will buy $1,000,000 in government bonds." So the government takes pieces of paper, paints official looking designs on them, and calls them treasury bonds. Then they put a value on the bonds to a sum of $1,000,000 and sends them to the Federal Reserve. The Fed then makes their own paper and calls them Federal Reserve notes. These notes are of equal value to the bonds. The notes are traded for bonds and received by the government. The government gets these notes and deposits them in the bank. These notes become money, adding $1,000,000 to the U.S. money supply.[82]

Only they now transact money electronically. Only 3% of the entire money supply is actual paper money, the rest is just numbers stored in computers.[83] When the government gets a loan, they are promising to pay back that money to the Federal Reserve at interest. Since the money issued to them is the money they need to pay back at interest, the U.S. government can never pay off the interest owed to the Federal Reserve.[84]

---

[82] https://www.community-exchange.org/docs/ModernMoneyMechanics.pdf
[83] http://positivemoney.org/how-money-works/how-banks-create-money/
[84] http://money.howstuffworks.com/how-much-money-is-in-the-world.htm

Therefore, they are always in debt to the Federal Reserve. In our society, money is equal to debt.

Banks are responsible for the circulation of money in our society. Money is stored in banks and it is distributed by banks. But a bank is also a business and businesses need to make money. So how do banks make their money? Banks make their money from selling loans to the public. The more loans the bank makes, the more money they make.

There are two types of people who visit banks: those who save their money in the bank, and those who want to borrow money from the bank. The bank makes loans to the people who want money the same money that others give to the banks to save. Because in our modern banking system, banks are only required to keep a certain percentage—a fraction—of the money you deposit in the bank, and can lend out the rest to make money with. This practice is called 'Fractional Reserve Banking,' which translates to mean "lending out many times more money than you have assets on deposit."

Today, banks are allowed to loan out at least ten times the amount they actually are holding, so while you wonder how they get rich charging you 11% interest, it's not 11% a year they make on that amount but actually 110%. The bank lends other people's money to those that need loans, and when the bank runs out of money, they call the Federal Reserve for more.

The Federal Reserve is a private bank that creates and controls the money in our country. By "private" I don't just mean that it is off limits to the public. No one is allowed to enter the Federal Reserve. Not the president, the Supreme Court, Congress, the FBI, the CIA, DOD, DEA—no one.[85] This private bank distributes money to private stockholders. They give loans to

[85] http://www.globalresearch.ca/who-owns-the-federal-reserve/10489

other banks, and the banks need to pay back the loans with interest. The U.S. Treasury was established to create the money for our country, but after many attempts to dominate our nation's currency, the bankers finally succeeded in 1913.

Chapter 17. The History of the Banking System

By taking a look back at history, we can easily come to understand how the elite gained so much control over society, and what their motives are. The people in power do not care about the power of the people. They care about control, they do not want people to be smart or independent, they want them to be good workers, obedient and unaware.

Money has always been a tool used to control the people. It did not evolve from thousands of years of barter and trade like we are led to believe; the priest-kings of ancient Sumer first introduced it. Written in the Sumerian tablets (the oldest written and deciphered record of human history), is a financial transaction of depositing silver shekels at the palace temple. It is one of the earliest examples of a "Bill of Exchange" used by modern banks, and tells us that temples in antiquity served as the first banks, creating a link between bankers and royal bloodlines as far back as we can trace.[86]

Every civilization has had a form of currency, usually silver and gold, that is controlled by the rulers and kings of that society. The people in power remain in power by controlling the circulation of money. It is no different today than it was thousands of years ago. Though money has been used as a tool of oppression, the real corruption of the monetary system began with the process of fractional reserve banking.

---

[86] http://www.investopedia.com/articles/07/banking.asp

Fractional reserve banking began around the 10th century, when goldsmiths began offering to keep other people's gold and silver safe in their vaults, and in return people would walk away with a receipt for what they had left there.[87] These paper receipts soon became popular for trade, as they were lighter to carry around than gold and silver coins. After a while, one goldsmith noticed that only a small percentage of their depositor's ever came in to demand their gold at any one time. So, cleverly, the goldsmith made out some receipts for gold that didn't even exist, and then they loaned it out to earn interest.

The people deposited their gold coins and received a note that assured them they could retrieve their gold whenever they wanted. If people deposited 100 gold coins, they would receive a note worth 100 gold coins on it. The idea was simple but lead to conflict when people began raising the price of their products. The inflation made the receipts worth less and less until they were not worth anything.

When everyone who had deposited gold decided that they wanted their money back, the goldsmith fled because he had no more gold to offer. The people were furious. They hunted the man down and hung him. Although the thief was dead, an evil invention was born: the idea of how to make money out of nothing. Like the atomic bomb, this was too much power to belong in the hands of irresponsible human beings.

Fractional reserve banking is the practice whereby a bank holds reserves in an amount equal to only a portion of the amount of its

---

[87] https://www.khanacademy.org/economics-finance-domain/macroeconomics/monetary-system-topic/fractional-reserve-banking-tut/v/overview-of-fractional-reserve-banking

customers' deposits, to satisfy potential demands for withdrawals. Reserves are held at the bank as currency, or as deposits reflected in the bank's accounts at the central bank. A bank makes its money by giving out loans. The banks give out more loans than money stored in their supply. If all of the banks customers wanted their money back at the same time, the bank would not be able to supply them with the money that is rightfully theirs.

To understand precisely how fractional reserve banking can be seen as fraudulent, just consider if I were to sell my car to two different drivers where both are under the impression that they had full use of the vehicle at any given time. Because both can't have access to the car at the same time, the crime of contractual fraud was committed. In the case of fractional reserve banking, if depositors were to agree that their money was to be used for additional lending, there would be no issue. But usually depositors don't fully realize that their funds are not really there in whole. Whether or not one regards fractional reserve banking as a clear case of fraud, it seems that a good portion of the public is wrongly informed on the mechanics of modern-day banking.[88]

Fractional reserve banking originated when bankers realized that not all depositors demand payment at the same time. In the past, savers looking to keep their coins and valuables in safekeeping depositories deposited gold and silver at goldsmiths, receiving in exchange a note for their deposit. These notes gained acceptance as a medium of exchange for commercial transactions and thus became an early form of circulating paper money.

---

[88] https://www.mises.ca/john-tamny-and-the-problem-with-fractional-reserve-banking/

Starting in the late 1600s, nations began to establish central banks, which were given the legal power to set the reserve requirement and to specify the required form in which such assets were to be held.[89]

In 1743, a goldsmith named Amshall Moses Bower opened a counting house in Frankfurt Germany. He placed a Roman eagle on a red shield over the door prompting people to call his shop the Red Shield Firm pronounced in German as "Rothschild."[90] His son later changed his name to Rothschild when he inherited the business. Loaning money to individuals was profitable but he soon found it much more profitable to loan money to governments and kings. It involved much bigger amounts, always secured from public taxes. Once he established a good financial foundation, he set his sights on the world by training his five sons in the art of money creation, before sending them out to the major financial centers of the world to create and dominate the central banking systems.

By the mid 1700's Britain was at its height of power, but was also heavily in debt. Since the creation of the Bank of England, they had suffered four costly wars and the total debt stood at £140,000,000. In order to make their interest payments to the bank, the British government decided to raise revenues from their American colonies, largely through an extensive series of taxation.

There was a shortage of material for minting coins in the colonies, so they began to print their own paper money, which they called colonial script. This provided a very successful method of exchange. Colonial script

---

[89] http://www.wikinvest.com/wiki/Central_Bank

[90] http://www.menwithfoilhats.com/2010/03/the-history-of-the-rothschild-banking-empire/

was money provided to help the exchange of goods. It was debt-free paper money not backed by gold or silver.[91]

Colonial script was issued in proper proportion to the demands of trade and industry, making it easy for products to pass from producers to consumers. The debt-free paper money caused the American colonies to thrive. They issued their own currency, which had no connection to the British government, preventing them from excessive taxation.

In response, the powerful Bank of England influenced British parliament to press for the passing of the Currency Act of 1764. This act made it illegal for the colonies to print their own money, and forced them to pay all future taxes to Britain in silver or gold.

Unsatisfied with the act, the American colonies rebelled against Britain, resulting in the war known today as the American Revolution. By the time the war began on April 19, 1775, much of the gold and silver had been taken by British taxation. The colonies were left with no other choice but to print money to finance the war. Colonial Script was so efficient that it became a threat to the established economic system of the time.[92]

The idea of issuing money in proper proportion to the demands of trade and industry, without charging interest, caused no problems and no inflation. This concept was unfamiliar to the Bank of England, which only issued money for the sake of making profit for its shareholders.

In 1781, arms dealer Robert Morris suggested he be allowed to set up a central bank in the USA. He proposed to deposit $400,000, allowing him

---

[91] http://www.kamron.com/liberty/colonial_script.htm

[92] http://www.factmonster.com/ipka/A0801059.html

to loan out many times that through fractional reserve banking.[93] Desperate for money, the impoverished American Government agreed.

Once in, he simply used fractional reserve banking to loan to himself and his friends the money to buy up all of the bank's remaining shares. The bank then began to loan out money multiplied by this new amount to eager politicians. The scam lasted until 1785, with the value of American money rapidly decreasing. The bank's charter didn't get renewed.[94] The shareholders walking off with the interest did not go unnoticed by the Founding Fathers.

> *"The rich will strive to establish their dominion and enslave the rest. They always did. They always will... They will have the same effect here as elsewhere, if we do not, by the power of government, keep them in their proper spheres."*
> *– Governor Morris, American statesman and Founding Father of the U.S.*

In 1791, the First Bank of the United States (BUS) was created.[95] The bank was not only misleadingly named to sound official, but also to take attention away from the real first bank, which had been shut down.

The American government borrowed 8.2 million dollars from the bank within the first 5 years. Inflation caused the prices to rise by 72%. The

---

[93] https://books.google.com/books?id=VbFEaef6YKQC&pg=PA63&lpg=PA63&dq=In+1781,+arms+dealer+Robert+Morris+suggested+he+be+allowed+to+set+up+a+central+bank+in+the+USA.+He&source=bl&ots=ZmzgGTr8KR&sig=kZ5cFhOIfcPQg_6zf-XYOnfY138&hl=en&sa=X&ved=0ahUKEwi2sMeNuvrJAhVExWMKHaRbDkAQ6AEIJDAC#v=onepage&q=In%201781%2C%20arms%20dealer%20Robert%20Morris%20suggested%20he%20be%20allowed%20to%20set%20up%20a%20central%20bank%20in%20the%20USA.%20He&f=false

[94] http://www.xat.org/xat/moneyhistory.html

[95] http://www.ushistory.org/tour/first-bank.htm

president, who could see an ever-increasing debt, was against the mischievous nature of central banks.[96]

> *"I wish it were possible to obtain a single amendment to our Constitution - taking from the federal government their power of borrowing."*
>
> *– Thomas Jefferson, the 3rd president of the United States*

As with the real first bank, the government had been the only depositor to contribute any real money, with the remainder being raised from loans the investors made to each other, using the magic of fractional reserve banking. When the time came for renewal of the charter, again the bankers were denied.

In 1816, the Rothschilds backed a privately owned central bank called the Second Bank of The United States.[97] In 1832, President Andrew Jackson ordered the withdrawal of government deposits from the second bank and instead put them into safe banks. Because the U.S. government was the largest shareholder of the Second Bank of The United States, this caused a huge problem with the bank's head. The Second Bank's head, Nicholas Biddle, was candid about the power and intention of the bank when he openly threatened to cause a depression if the bank was not re-chartered.

---

[96] http://www.xat.org/xat/moneyhistory.html

[97] http://www.let.rug.nl/usa/essays/general/a-brief-history-of-central-banking/second-bank-of-the-united-states-%281816-1836%29.php

"Nothing but widespread suffering will produce any effect on Congress...Our only safety is in pursuing a steady course of firm restriction – and I have no doubt that such a course will ultimately lead to the restoration of the currency and the re-charter of the bank."

– Nicholas Biddle

In 1836, when the charter ran out, the Second Bank ceased to function. When asked what the greatest achievement of his career was, Andrew Jackson replied, "I killed the bank!" Although the financial influence of private banks was not over.

With the Central Bank killed off, fractional reserve banking moved rapidly through numerous state-chartered banks, causing the instability that this form of economics thrives on. Privately owned banks issued paper currency in the form of banknotes, the notes being redeemable for silver or gold coins at the bank's office. They were not legal tender. Such notes had value only if the bank could be counted on to redeem them. If a bank failed, its notes became worthless.

President Lincoln, needing money to finance his war effort, printed 450 million dollars in new bills using green ink on the back to distinguish them from the other notes. These notes were called "greenbacks." They were not backed by gold or silver. Instead, they were backed by the credibility of the U.S. Government.[98]

"The government should create, issue and circulate all the currency and credit needed to satisfy the spending power of the government and the buying power of consumers...The privilege of creating and issuing money is not only the supreme prerogative of

---

[98] http://www.garynorth.com/public/6875.cfm

government, but it is the government's greatest creative opportunity. By the adoption of these principles, the long-felt want for a uniform medium will be satisfied. The taxpayers will be saved immense sums of interest, discounts and exchanges. The financing of all public enterprises, the maintenance of stable government and ordered progress, and the conduct of the Treasury will become matters of practical administration. The people can and will be furnished with a currency as safe as their own government. Money will cease to be the master and become the servant of humanity. Democracy will rise superior to the money power."

– Abraham Lincoln

This solution worked so well, Lincoln considered adopting the emergency measure as a permanent policy. This would have been great for everyone except the moneychangers, who quickly realized how dangerous this policy would be for them. With Government supplying its own money without cost, all debts would be paid off and none would be created. It would become the most prosperous country, and a threat to the fractional reserve banking system that gave the banks so much power.

In 1863, Lincoln needed more money to support the Civil War. Although there were only 450 million greenbacks in circulation, Lincoln couldn't get the congressional authority to issue more. Taking advantage of this, the bankers proposed the passing of the National Bank Act. The act went through and the U.S. money supply returned to being created out of debt by bankers buying U.S. bonds and issuing bank notes.[99]

[99] http://www.let.rug.nl/usa/essays/general/a-brief-history-of-central-banking/national-banking-acts-of-1863-and-1864.php

The North won the Civil War and Lincoln attempted to reverse the act he had been pressured to sign during the war. He would have succeeded if he had not been assassinated 41 days after being re-elected.

Now, the Lincoln memorial in Washington D.C. faces a building called the Federal Reserve Headquarters. This institution would not be here if Lincoln's monetary policy had been adopted. The Federal Reserve is not actually "federal;" the name is designed to give the appearance that it is operating in the public's interest, when it is actually a privately held organization run solely to gain profit for select stockholders.

The Federal Reserve came into existence On December 23, 1913 when the House of Representatives passed the Federal Reserve Act. With the passing of this act, Congress required that all nationally chartered banks become members of the Federal Reserve System. These banks were required to purchase specified non-transferable stock in their regional Federal Reserve banks, and to set aside a stipulated amount of non-interest bearing reserves with their respective reserve banks.[100]

Each dollar that is added to the money supply must be paid back by the U.S. Government with interest, and each time the money supply increases, the value of the money decreases. This is the system that is used to severely damage a nation's economy for the profit and gain of a few bankers.

The Federal Reserve Act was signed by President Woodrow Wilson, an accomplice of the bankers who had agreed to sign the act before he was even in office. After signing the act Wilson realized what he had done:

---

[100] https://www.corbettreport.com/federalreserve/

> *"I am a most unhappy man. I have unwittingly ruined my country. A great industrial nation is controlled by its system of credit. Our system of credit is concentrated. The growth of the nation, therefore, and all our activities are in the hands of a few men. We have come to be one of the worst ruled, one of the most completely controlled and dominated Governments in the civilized world. No longer a Government by free opinion, no longer a Government by conviction and the vote of the majority, but a Government by the opinion and duress of a small group of dominant men."*
>
> *– Woodrow Wilson, the 28th president of the United States*

Since 1913, the Federal Reserve has been robbing the United States of a healthy economy. Every dollar printed creates debt and requires more money to pay off the debt. Adding more money to the supply decreases its value, resulting in inflation. Fractional Reserve banking has caused the collapse of many great nations, and if we continue to allow it to have monetary control, it will be the collapse of our nation as well.

The Federal Reserve is a central bank established in the United States, but almost every country in the world has an established central bank, each of which is owned by the Rothschild family. There are only three countries left in the world without an established Rothschild central bank. These countries are Cuba, North Korea, and Iran, which are coincidentally countries we have much conflict with.[101]

Central banks are creating world monopolization by controlling the money supply. Mayer Amschel Rothschild, the founder of the House of

---

101 http://www.fourwinds10.net/siterun_data/government/banking_and_taxation_irs_and_insurance/social_security/news.php?q=1320062234

Rothschild, even said, "Let me issue and control a nation's money and I care not who writes the laws."

The power of central banks affects the entire world, but their true rise to power began after the establishment of the Federal Reserve.

Chapter 18. The Banks' Rise to Power

In 1901, Nikola Tesla, an inventor, electrical engineer, and one of the greatest minds in history, began working on a project called the Wardenclyffe Tower. The purpose of the tower was to supply free energy to the world. It was a method of broadcasting electrical energy without wires. Wealthy banker J.P. Morgan initially backed the project, investing $150,000 in the facility, although at the time, J.P. Morgan was not informed of Tesla's intention of providing free energy. By 1903, Tesla's project, still under construction due to numerous design changes, ran out of money and Morgan declined to fund it any further.[102]

It was at this point that Tesla sent a series of letters to J.P. Morgan soliciting additional funding for the project, despite the fact that Morgan had already warned Tesla with his initial investment that he would provide no further financing. In Tesla's third letter to Morgan in 1903, he finally revealed his intent to use the facility to transmit wireless power, saying "...If I would have told you such as this before, you would have fired me out of your office... Will you help me or let my great work—almost complete—go to pots?..." Morgan responded on July 14th "I have received your letter... and in reply would say that I should not feel disposed at present to make any further advances."

The Wardenclyffe Tower project was shut down and all of Tesla's documents were seized by J.P. Morgan. If it were not for this powerful

---

[102] https://www.pbs.org/tesla/ll/ll_todre.html

banker, the entire world would be supplied with free energy. This does not involve the Federal Reserve, but it is a good example of how banks have limited human potential. J.P. Morgan did not finance Tesla's tower because he saw it as a threat to the existing energy companies. There was no way to make a profit from an abundance of free energy. This greed for profit and power is what is holding us back as a species.

Henry Ford, an American Industrialist and the founder of Ford Motor Company, told a New York Times reporter in 1925 that ethyl alcohol was "the fuel of the future." He was expressing an opinion that was widely shared in the automotive industry. "The fuel of the future is going to come from fruit like that sumac out by the road, or from apples, weeds, sawdust -- almost anything," he said. "There is fuel in every bit of vegetable matter that can be fermented. There's enough alcohol in one year's yield of an acre of potatoes to drive the machinery necessary to cultivate the fields for a hundred years."[103]

When Henry Ford designed the Model T, it was his expectation that ethanol, made from renewable biological materials, would be a major automobile fuel. However, gasoline emerged as the dominant transportation fuel in the early twentieth century because of the ease of operation of gasoline engines with the materials then available for engine construction. Many bills proposing a national energy program that made use of America's vast agricultural resources for fuel production were killed by smear campaigns launched by vested petroleum interests.[104] The oil

---

[103] http://www.environmentalhistory.org/billkovarik/about-bk/research/henry-ford-charles-kettering-and-the-fuel-of-the-future/

[104] http://rense.com/general67/ford.htm

companies had a monopoly over the automobile industry, and creating a new fuel would be a threat to their power. Due to the threat ethanol fuel posed to major oil companies, production was shut down and the idea of using ethanol as fuel became a thing of the past, another example of how the greed of power and profit has limited our potential.

From 1929 to 1933 the Federal Reserve contracted the amount of currency in circulation by one-third. This contraction of money resulted in the economic crash known as The Great Depression. The father of the Federal Reserve, Paul Warburg, warned investors of the coming collapse and depression. All of the Wall Street giants, including J.P. Morgan, Joe F. Kennedy, J.D. Rockefeller, and Bernard Baruch, got out of the stock market and put their assets into gold just before the crash. Forty billion dollars vanished during the crash (although, it did not really vanish, it simply shifted into the hands of the bankers). This is how Joe Kennedy went from having $4 million dollars in 1929 to having over $100 million in 1935.[105]

"It was not accidental. It was a carefully contrived occurrence...The international bankers sought to bring about a condition of despair here so that they might emerge as rulers of us all."

– Congressman Louis T. McFadden (D-PA), who served twelve years as Chairman of the Committee on Banking and Currency

[105] https://criminalbankingmonopoly.wordpress.com/

Most people are aware of Adolf Hitler and his rise to power. What most people do not know is that he was almost completely financed by money drawn from the privately owned American Federal Reserve.[106]

> *"After WWI, Germany fell into the hands of the international bankers. Those bankers bought her and they now own her, lock, stock, and barrel. They have purchased her industries, they have mortgages on her soil, they control her production, they control all her public utilities. The international German bankers have subsidized the present Government of Germany and they have also supplied every dollar of the money Adolf Hitler has used in his lavish campaign to build up threat to the government of Bruening. When Bruening fails to obey the orders of the German International Bankers, Hitler is brought forth to scare the Germans into submission... Through the Federal Reserve Board over $30 billion of American money has been pumped into Germany. You have all heard of the spending that has taken place in Germany... Modernistic dwellings, her great planetariums, her gymnasiums, her swimming pools, her fine public highways, her perfect factories. All this was done on our money. All this was given to Germany through the Federal Reserve Board. The Federal Reserve Board has pumped so many billions of dollars into Germany that they dare not name the total."*
>
> *– Congressman Louis T. McFadden*

During World War II, the United States' debt increased by 598%, Japan's debt increased by 1,348%, France's debt increased by 583%, and Canada's debt increased by 417%. The central banks fund every Government for war. War is the biggest way for the banks to gain profit. The Governments need

[106] http://www.reformed-theology.org/html/books/wall_street/chapter_07.htm

money to supply the war, and the banks supply them, knowing that they are funding to separate competitors in the same war.[107]

Just after WWI, the bankers were attempting to consolidate the central banks under the guise of peacemaking. To stop future wars, they put forward the formation of a world central bank named the Bank of International Settlements, a world court called the World Court in The Hague, and a world executive for legislation called the League of Nations. In his 1966 book entitled Tragedy and Hope, President Clinton's mentor Carroll Quigley writes about this:

> *"The powers of financial capitalism had a far-reaching plan, nothing less than to create a world system of financial control in private hands able to dominate the political system of each country and the economy of the world as a whole. This system was to be controlled in a feudalist fashion by the central banks of the world acting in concert, by secret agreements arrived at in frequent meetings and conferences. The apex of the system was to be the Bank for International Settlements in Basel, Switzerland, a private bank owned and controlled by the world's central banks which were themselves private corporations. Each central bank... sought to dominate its government by its ability to control treasury loans, to manipulate foreign exchanges, to influence the level of economic activity in the country, and to influence cooperative politicians by subsequent economic rewards in the business world."*
>
> *– Professor Carroll Quigley,*
> *Georgetown University*

---

[107] https://www.linkedin.com/pulse/money-changers-part-iii-global-nations-see-writing-wall-cheryl-king?trkSplashRedir=true&forceNoSplash=true

They got two out of three. The League of Nations failed, largely owing to the suspicions of the people, and while opposition focused on this, the other two proposals snuck their way through. In 1944, the U.S. approved its full participation in the International Monetary Fund (IMF) and the World Bank. By 1945, the second League of Nations was approved under the new name "The United Nations." The war had dissolved all opposition. The methods used in the National Banking Act of 1864 and the Federal Reserve Act of 1913 were now simply used on a global scale.

The Federal Reserve Act, allowing the creation of Federal Reserve notes, is mirrored by the IMF's authority to produce money, called Special Drawing Rights (SDR).[108] It is estimated that the IMF has produced thirty billion dollars' worth of SDRs so far. In the United States, SDRs are already accepted as legal money, and all other member nations are being pressured to follow suit. With SDRs being partially backed by gold, a world gold standard is sneaking its way in through the back door, which comes with no objection from the bankers who now hold two-thirds of the world's gold and can use this to structure the world's economy to their further advantage.

The last attempt to end the Federal Reserve was by President John F. Kennedy. On June 4, 1963, Executive Order 11110 was signed with the authority to strip the Federal Reserve Bank of its power to loan money to the United States Federal Government at interest. With the stroke of a pen, President Kennedy declared that the privately owned Federal Reserve Bank would soon be out of business.

When President John Fitzgerald Kennedy signed this Order, it returned to the federal government, specifically the Treasury Department, the

---

[108] http://www.imf.org/external/np/exr/facts/sdr.htm

Constitutional power to create and issue currency without going through the privately owned Federal Reserve Bank. President Kennedy's Executive Order 11110 gave the Treasury Department the explicit authority "to issue silver certificates against any silver bullion, silver, or standard silver dollars in the Treasury." This means that for every ounce of silver in the U.S. Treasury's vault, the government could introduce new money into circulation based on the silver bullion physically held there. As a result, more than $4 billion in United States Notes were brought into circulation in $2 and $5 denominations.[109]

"We are opposed around the world by a monolithic and ruthless conspiracy that relies primarily on covert means for expanding its sphere of influence — on infiltration instead of invasion — on subversion instead of elections — on intimidation instead of free choice — on guerrillas by night instead of armies by day. It is a system which has conscripted vast human and material resources into the building of a tightly-knit, highly efficient machine that combines military, diplomatic, intelligence, economic, scientific and political operations. Its preparations are concealed, not published. Its mistakes are buried, not headlined. Its dissenters are silenced, not praised. No expenditure is questioned, no rumor is printed, no secret is revealed. No president should fear public scrutiny of his program. For from that scrutiny comes understanding; and from that understanding comes support or opposition. And both are necessary. I am not asking your newspapers to support the Administration, but I am asking your help in the tremendous task of informing and alerting the American

[109] http://www.john-f-kennedy.net/thefederalreserve.htm

people. For I have complete confidence in the response and dedication of our citizens whenever they are fully informed."
– John F. Kennedy

President Kennedy gave this speech on April 27, 1961 in an address before the American Newspaper Publishers Association. From the moment of his election, JFK intended to shut down the central banks. After executive order 11110 was signed in June 1963, his goal was nearly accomplished. Unfortunately, four months later, on November 22, 1963, President John F. Kennedy was assassinated. Vice President Lyndon B. Johnson assumed the presidency after Kennedy's assassination in 1963. Just two months after Kennedy's assassination, in his first economic report to Congress, Johnson recommended that America "expedite the release of silver from the coinage." Johnson discontinued the issuance of silver certificates in 1964, and the process of retiring the outstanding certificates began, supporting the Federal Reserve's agenda.

JFK was the last President to oppose the power of central banks. From that point in time the Federal Reserve has continued to increase its power, having control over all Federal institutions, corporations, and major media outlets.

If we want a healthy economy, we need the issuing of money to return to the government and not to be a power of private banks. We need money backed by real valuable goods, not pieces of paper that must be paid back at interest. Money is supposed to benefit humanity, not make us its servant.

Chapter 19. Maintaining Public Ignorance

To ensure the obedience of the American people, many actions have been taken by the Federal Government to keep the public misinformed, uneducated, and ignorant of the monetary situation. The civil rights movement was one of the biggest threats to government influence.

In 1956, The FBI created the Counter-Intelligence Program (COINTELPRO).[110] The program was developed as a series of covert operations aimed at surveying, infiltrating, discrediting, and disrupting domestic political organizations. Though the program ended in 1971, similar tactics are still used to this day, and have been alleged to include discrediting targets through psychological warfare; smearing individuals and groups using forged documents and by planting false reports in the media; harassment; wrongful imprisonment; and illegal violence, including assassination.[111] This program was most active during the civil rights movement, and plays a huge part in the untold history of the world.

Martin Luther King, Jr. was targeted and killed in 1968. In 1999, during a civil court case, the U.S. government was proven guilty for his death.[112] Even Albert Einstein, who was a member of several civil rights groups, was under FBI surveillance.[113] FBI Director J. Edgar Hoover ordered FBI agents

---

[110] https://vault.fbi.gov/cointel-pro

[111] http://www.amazon.com/Tupac-Shakur-Black-Leaders-Intelligences/dp/0979146909

[112] http://www.washingtonsblog.com/2015/01/martin-luther-king-assassinated-us-govt-king-family-civil-trial-verdict.html

[113] https://www.wsws.org/en/articles/2002/09/eins-s03.html

to "expose, disrupt, misdirect, discredit, neutralize, or otherwise eliminate" the activities of domestic political organizations.

During the Black Panther movement, African-American communities were flooded with heroin, eventually leading to the fall of the Black Panther party. The FBI is still using tactics of counter-intelligence today.[114]

Psychological warfare has been a method of keeping the public uneducated, and has had a major influence on the population for generations. Imagine where we would be today if this program did not exist.

Another program aimed at maintaining public ignorance was the CIA's Project MK-Ultra. Project MK-Ultra, sometimes referred to as the CIA's mind control program, is the code name of a U.S. Government human research operation experimenting in the behavioral engineering of humans.[115] Organized through the Scientific Intelligence Division of the CIA, the project coordinated with the Special Operations Division of the U.S. Army's Chemical Corps. The program engaged in many illegal activities; in particular it used unwitting U.S. and Canadian citizens as its test subjects, which led to controversy regarding its legitimacy. MK-Ultra used numerous methods to manipulate people's mental states and alter brain functions, including the secretive administration of drugs and other chemicals, hypnosis, sensory deprivation, isolation, verbal and sexual abuse, as well as various forms of torture.[116]

The scope of Project MK-Ultra was broad, with research undertaken at 80 institutions, including 44 colleges and universities, as well as hospitals,

---

[114] http://intelnews.org/2013/12/19/01-1390/

[115] http://www.todayifoundout.com/index.php/2013/09/one-shocking-cia-programs-time-project-mkultra/

[116] http://www.mindspring.com/~txporter/sec3.htm

prisons and pharmaceutical companies. The CIA operated through these institutions using front organizations, although sometimes, top officials at these institutions were aware of the CIA's involvement.[117]

Project MK-Ultra practiced what is known as Monarch Mind Control. Monarch Mind Control (MMC) is a form of mind control that creates a mind control slave by utilizing the human brain's trauma response of dissociation to create a form of Multiple Personality Disorder (MPD), wherein various triggers can cause the slave personality to surface and respond to commands given by the master.[118]

The Monarch Mind Control designation was originally applied by the U.S. Department of Defense to a sub-program under the CIA's MK-Ultra Program. However, the techniques employed in the Monarch programming system extend back further under various names, such as the Nazi marionette programming.[119] Even further back, the techniques used in Monarch programming can be traced to various generational Satanist families among European royalty.

MMC utilizes a combination of psychology, neuroscience, and occult rituals to create within the slaves an alter persona that can be triggered and programmed by the handlers. Monarch slaves are used by several organizations connected with the world elite in fields such as the military, sex slavery, and the entertainment industry. The purpose of this horrible program is to control the mind of individuals who have public influence. As

---

[117] http://www.wanttoknow.info/770804nytimes.ciabehaviorcontrolmk-ultra

[118] http://vigilantcitizen.com/hidden-knowledge/origins-and-techniques-of-monarch-mind-control/

[119] http://www.bibliotecapleyades.net/sociopolitica/esp_sociopol_mindcon02.htm

terrifying as this sounds, the program is real, and is responsible for much of the public ignorance apparent in our society.

The select stockholders of the private central banks have the most influence over the world. They control the economic situation of our society and influence the decisions made by political leaders. They have gained so much power by remaining a secret to the general population, even though most of the corruption our society experiences can be traced back to the few rich and powerful bankers.

The banks have power over the corporations. In a capitalist society, the corporations have the most capital (money), and therefore they have the most influence. Presidential elections are funded by corporations, and in return the elected officials serve the interest of the corporations that supported them.[120] [121] [122]

The corporations control everything in our society. They have control of our governments, water, energy, food, media – the resources that we depend on for survival are controlled and managed by large corporations.

Six corporations rule the dominant information flows in our society. They decide the stories that get told and the stories that don't. The corporations are General Electric (GE), which owns NBC, Universal, and Focus Features; Viacom, which owns MTV, Nickelodeon, BET, and Paramount; News Corp, which owns Fox, The Wall Street Journal, and the New York Post; Time Warner, which owns CNN, HBO, Time, Warner Bros, & DC; CBS, which owns Showtime, Smithsonian, NFL, and 60 Minutes; and

---

[120] http://listverse.com/2015/05/28/10-real-victims-of-the-cias-mkultra-program/
[121] http://www.mindspring.com/~txporter/sec3.htm
[122] http://vigilantcitizen.com/hidden-knowledge/origins-and-techniques-of-monarch-mind-control/

Disney, which owns ABC, ESPN, Marvel, Miramax, and Pixar. Each of these house hundreds of thousands of regional corporations and services worldwide. [123] [124]

The same six corporations own the media outlets that we rely on for nearly all of our information. These corporations serve the interest of the central banks. The strength of these corporations lies in the large amounts of money that they generate. If the people were informed of the control these corporations have, then they would stop investing their money towards these companies, and the corporations would lose their power and wealth. It is in the best interest of the government, the corporations and the banks to keep the public uninformed. The biggest tool of maintaining public ignorance is by the control of media outlets that distribute information to the mass population.

When the media puts on a week of breaking news on Justin Bieber, the Kardashians, or any other popular celebrity, while it has a total blackout on world revolutions and innovations that can change the world – you know the reason why. If it is against the interest of the banks and corporations, then the media will not discuss it.

Not only is information suppressed and reformed through the media, but it is also controlled by the educational system. When a child is born, they have no state of mind or prior beliefs. Their mind is a blank canvas, pure consciousness ready to experience and create life. They learn by

---

123 http://investmentwatchblog.com/only-six-corporations-own-all-mainstream-media-in-the-united-states/

124 http://www.businessinsider.com/these-6-corporations-control-90-of-the-media-in-america-2012-6

observing the things around them, and are raised to be a product of their environment.

When you were young, your mother said, "table, chair, door, bird, mom, dad" over and over again until it became a part of how you think. Even hatred, racial discrimination, and envy are taught to children by the culture. Our behavior is learned. No Chinese child is born speaking Chinese; they learn that from their parents or whom they grow up with.

Plants do not grow all by themselves; they are fueled by the sunlight, the soil, and all of the other factors required for their development. A sailboat does not sail; the wind moves the sail. All things are influenced by something else, as all people are acted upon by other things. Our behavior is generated by the many interacting variables that we encounter; there is no one thing that influences human behavior.

When the bankers in power get control of the things that shape our behavior, they start to have more control over our lives. Media outlets are controlled, food, water, and energy are controlled, and the educational system that raises our children is controlled. They control society and the way that it functions through their influence over the factors that form our behavior.

For the first few years of a child's life they are taught how to speak, walk, eat and learn other necessary survival skills. By the time they are smart enough to begin thinking critically, they are placed in a mandatory institution. Our whole lives are influenced by institutions. Schools, Federal organizations, media outlets, corporations, are all institutions that have a major influence over a child's development in the modern world.

Once the child is placed in a learning institution, they are told that they will become successful by completing school, going to college, and getting a career. They start by learning basic things such as coloring in the lines and recognizing shapes. Then they move on to kindergarten to learn more. When kindergarten is completed they move to the first grade. Then to second grade, then third, fourth and so on until they complete grade school and move on to high school.

Now they are getting closer to that success they have been promised. Once high school is completed they move on to college, and even graduate school. Once they complete that, they get to move out into the world. By that time, they likely already have a load of debt, student loans, financial aid, car payments, food, housing, etc., and are forced to find a job so that they can afford to live. Then they get sucked into some corporate job where they have a quota to make, or a promotion to accomplish. They work hard for a few years and move up in the company, then work harder for another few years to get the next promotion, so they can achieve the success that they have been assured. Then one day, when the child is about 40 years old, they arrive at that great success that they have strived for.

Once they are there, they realize that they feel no different than they have always felt. The whole thing was a game to distract them from living their life. By the time they realize it, they are too old to change it. We are taught that life is a journey with a serious purpose at the end, and the whole point is to reach that end, to accomplish success. But we miss the point. Life is an experience that we are supposed to enjoy as we live it, not wait until the moment we achieve success to feel content.

The child does not know better at the time they are placed in grade school. Everyone they look up to tells them that they need to follow this system or become a failure. Their behavior is molded by the influence of their environment and they become another member of our corrupt and ignorant society.

The educational system does not teach the child to be smart, loving, or independent. They are taught to be obedient, competitive, and valuable to the work force. They are taught how to train for a job, and how to be a successful worker. Keep in mind that the learning institutions are controlled by the rich and powerful people who do not want an educated public.

> *"I do not want a nation of thinkers,*
> *I want a nation of workers."*
> *–John D. Rockefeller, who created the General Education Board (GEB) in 1903*

The modern educational system teaches children how to obey authority. People are not being educated; they're being tested for levels of obedience. School is about memorizing what you are told short-term and repeating it. Children are taught that truth comes from authority, that intelligence is the ability to remember and repeat, that accurate memory and repetition are rewarded, that noncompliance is punished, and that they need to conform both intellectually and socially. The sad truth is, our educational system is flawed. It does not properly educate the people; it teaches them how to be good workers.

We cannot expect to get a proper education from our corrupt system. Sure, they may teach some valuable information (I am not saying that they are completely useless), but they do not teach human beings what human beings need to know in order to survive, because if they did, you would not be dependent upon the system that they have fabricated.

To understand Nature, and to have an appropriate education, you must educate yourself. Read books, read articles, watch documentaries, do research and only formulate opinions when you have hard evidence to back it up, and if it matches your own common sense. Most importantly, remain open-minded to all possibilities. It is your responsibility to form your own opinions, not to believe what the majority of people think, because sadly the majority of people do not know how to think critically.

"Self-education is, I firmly believe, the only kind of education there is."
— Isaac Asimov

Typically, if you do not have a degree from a prestigious school, then you are viewed as less intelligent or under-qualified. Universities charge a ridiculous amount for tuition, sometimes exceeding $20,000 per semester. The public schools are funded and controlled by elected officials, who serve the wealthy for funding their elections.[125] The entire educational system has been transformed into a business. In school you are taught how to be obedient. The goal for completing school is to get a job that will give you a livable salary. Most graduates depend on that salary to pay off the loans they were given for that overpriced tuition. We are trapped since day one, taught that a completely unnatural way of life is the only way to succeed amongst our peers.

"Only a fool would let the enemy teach their kids."
– Malcolm X

[125] http://lwv.org/content/role-federal-government-public-education-equity-and-funding

As a result of an entire population living this lifestyle, we have become ignorant to the natural world, the state of our society, and our true selves. By living such a negative lifestyle, we have become unaware of our effect on the world, and have given the power to people that wish nothing better for us than a life of servitude.

Living in an ignorant society, we have been taught how to consume products. The banks have made it so that money is a necessity to live, instead of being a means of exchanging goods. By frivolously consuming, we have contributed a great amount of waste to the planet. We abuse and pollute the resources that we depend on for our survival. Our air is contaminated, our water is contaminated, our food is contaminated, and essentially, we are contaminated due to our consumption of these contaminated resources.

George Carlin, a comedian well known for his intelligent and political humor, did an excellent job of putting our current situation into perspective. Below is a quote from one of his stand-up acts. I must warn you ahead of time that there is some explicit language in this quote:

> *"If you talk to one of them about this, if you isolate one of them, you sit 'em down rationally, you talk to 'em about the low IQ's and the dumb behavior and the bad decisions; right away they start talking about education. That's the big answer to everything: Education. They say, 'We need more money for education. We need more books, more teachers, more classrooms, more schools. We need more testing for the kids!' You say to 'em, 'Well, you know, we've tried all that and the kids still can't pass the tests'. They say, 'Aw, don't you worry about that, we're gonna lower the passing grades!' And that's what they do in a lot of these schools now, they lower the passing grades so more kids can pass. More kids pass, the school looks*

good, everybody's happy; the IQ of the country slips another two or three points and pretty soon, all you'll need to get into college is a fucking pencil! 'Got a pencil? Get the fuck in there, it's physics!' Then everyone wonders why 17 other countries graduate more scientists than we do. Education!

Politicians know that word; they use it on you. Politicians have traditionally hidden behind three things: the flag, the Bible and children. 'No Child Left Behind! No Child Left Behind!' 'Oh really, well it wasn't long ago you were talking about giving kids a Head Start! Head Start, Left Behind, someone's losing fucking ground here!' But there's a reason. There's a reason. There's a reason for this. There's a reason education sucks and it's the same reason it will never, ever, ever be fixed. It's never going to get any better, don't look for it, be happy with what you got. Because the owners of this country don't want that.

I'm talking about the real owners now. The big, wealthy...The real owners, the big wealthy business interests that control things and make all the important decisions. Forget the politicians, they're an irrelevancy. The politicians are put there to give you the idea that you have freedom of choice. You don't. You have no choice. You have owners. They own you. They own everything. They own all the important land. They own and control the corporations. They've long since bought and paid for the Senate, the Congress, the statehouses, the city halls. They've got the judges in their back pockets, and they own all the big media companies, so they control just about all of the news and information you get to hear. They've got you by the balls! They spend billions of dollars every year lobbying – lobbying to get what they want. Well, we know what they want; they want more for themselves and less for everybody else.

But I'll tell you what they don't want. They don't want a population of citizens capable of critical thinking. They don't want well-informed, well-educated people capable of critical thinking.

They're not interested in that! That doesn't help them. That's against their interests. That's right! You know something? They don't want people who are smart enough to sit around the kitchen table and figure out how badly they're getting fucked by a system that threw them overboard 30 fucking years ago. They don't want that! You know what they want? They want Obedient Workers – Obedient Workers. People who are just smart enough to run the machines and do the paperwork but just dumb enough to passively accept all these increasingly shittier jobs with the lower pay, the longer hours, the reduced benefits, the end of overtime and the vanishing pension that disappears the minute you go to collect it. And, now, they're coming for your Social Security money. They want your fucking retirement money. They want it back, so they can give it to their criminal friends on Wall Street. And you know something? They'll get it. They'll get it all from you, sooner or later, because they own this fucking place. It's a big club - and you ain't in it! You and I are not in the big club.

By the way, it's the same big club they use to beat you over the head with all day long and they tell you what to believe...All day long, beating you over the head in the media, what to believe, what to think and what to buy...The table is tilted, folks! The game is rigged! And nobody seems to notice, and nobody seems to care! Good honest, hard-working people! White collar, blue collar... Doesn't matter what color shirt you have on! Good honest, hard-working people continue...These are people of modest means!...continue to elect these rich cocksuckers who don't give a fuck about them! They don't give a fuck about you! They don't give a fuck about you! They don't care about you! At all! At all! At all! Yeah! You know? And nobody seems to notice, nobody seems to care. That's what the owners count on. The fact that Americans probably will remain willfully ignorant of the big red white and blue dick that's being jammed up their assholes every day! Because the owners of this country know the truth—it's called the American Dream: because you have to be asleep to believe it."

– George Carlin

The people in power do NOT want us to expand our consciousness. If we begin to realize that we are powerful souls that create our reality, it will take away their power to enslave us. That is why there is fluoride in our water, chemicals in our air, and GMOs in our food. That is why we are bombarded with distractions to keep our minds occupied with things that don't matter. They don't want us to think at all.

Any act of rebellion toward the elite, even peaceful protest, is likely to result in the use of police or military force on public citizens.

America is slowly turning into a police state, along with many of the other countries controlled by the corrupt global banking system.

> *"In 1942, there were 110,000 Japanese American citizens in good standing, law-abiding people who were thrown into internment camps simply because their parents were born in the wrong country. That's all they did wrong. They had no right to a lawyer, no right to due process of any kind. The only right they had: "Right this way" into the internment camps! Just when these American citizens needed their rights the most, their government took them away! And rights aren't rights if someone else can take them away. They're privileges. That's all we've ever had in this country, is a bill of temporary privileges. And if you read the news even badly, you know that every year the list gets shorter and shorter and shorter."*
>
> *– George Carlin*

Chapter 20. A Totalitarian Regime

You may be familiar with the book *1984,* by George Orwell. Written in 1948, *1984* was George Orwell's frightening prophecy about the future. 1984 has come and gone, but Orwell's vision of a corrupt and oppressive society is alive and well. In the book, Big Brother refers to the tyrannical Party that "seeks power entirely for its own sake. We are not interested in the good of others; we are interested solely in power." His prediction of the future is remarkable in its accuracy. He prophesized the vision of a power-hungry government by paying attention to history and observing the direction that society was heading.

We can do the same, by studying our history and focusing on the motives of the elite, we can draw an image of what our future might look like, and if we stay on the current path that we are on, the future looks very grim.

"The Matrix is a system... that system is our enemy. But when you're inside, you look around, what do you see? Businessmen, teachers, lawyers, carpenters – the very minds of the people we are trying to save; But until we do, these people are still a part of that system and that makes them our enemy. You have to understand, most people are not ready to be unplugged. And many of them are so inured, so hopelessly dependent on the system that they will fight to protect it."

– Morpheus, from the movie "The Matrix"

The movie "The Matrix" is more than just an action-packed movie about robots taking over humanity; it is deeper than that. There is a message behind it, like there is in most movies, but the majority of people do not see things past face value. The analogy is that there is a world within the mind of the mass population, which controls the way they think and act, and that it is possible to see past that illusion, but you have to be willing to accept the truth (in reference to the movie, "taking the red pill").

The truth is always the truth, although if a lie has been repeated enough, especially by a figure of authority, the general population will begin to see those lies as truth. Look at Nazi Germany for instance: everything that Adolf Hitler did to the Jews during the time of the Holocaust was completely legal. The laws were created by the authority figures and the people blindly accepted them as truth, even though it was a disaster to humanity and killed millions of people.[126] It certainly went against all moral justifications of right and wrong, but under the laws of Germany in 1942, it was completely legal.

Fast-forward to today and you will see the same thing beginning in our society. The rights of the people are attacked, the right to own guns is questioned, and laws are enacted that deprive the people of their freedom.

The National Defense Authorization Act (NDAA) is a federal law specifying the budget and expenditures of the United States Department of Defense (DOD). Each year's act also includes other provisions, some related to civil liberties. The bill now says that detainees may be brought to the United States for "detention pursuant to the Authorization for Use of Military Force" (AUMF).[127] In plain English, that means the policy of indefinite detention by the military, without charge or trial, could now be legally carried out in the U.S.

---

[126] http://www.ushmm.org/wlc/en/article.php?ModuleId=10007887

[127] http://armedservices.house.gov/index.cfm/ndaa-home?p=ndaa

Another unconstitutional act is the Patriot Act, allowing the government to search and seize Americans' papers and effects without probable cause. "To assist terror investigation," the government may also monitor religious and political institutions without suspecting criminal activity. The government may monitor conversations between attorneys and clients in federal prisons and deny lawyers to Americans accused of crimes. The government may prosecute librarians or keepers of any other records if they tell anyone the government subpoenaed information related to a terror investigation.[128]

The rights listed in our constitution do not mean anything anymore to the Federal Government. The National Security Agency (NSA) spies on American citizens, taps our phones, and reads our emails.[129] There is a camera watching us on every street corner. America has been taken over by a totalitarian regime with an agenda for world domination. This is not the first time someone has tried to control the world, but it could be the last if we allow it to happen. As long as the people are aware, we can prevent it. But if people remain ignorant like they have for so long, this corrupt and unjust government will enslave us.

"A society whose citizens refuse to see and investigate the facts, who refuse to believe that their government and their media will routinely lie to them and fabricate a reality contrary to verifiable facts, is a society that chooses and deserves the police state dictatorship it is going to get."

—Ian Williams Goodard

---

[128] http://www.justice.gov/archive/ll/highlights.htm

[129] https://www.eff.org/nsa-spying

We think that something as bad as the holocaust could never happen again, but what we don't realize is that the holocaust did not just occur out of nowhere. The Nazi party slowly changed laws little by little until the rights of the people were taken away. Hitler himself even said,

> *"The best way to take control over a people and control them utterly is to take a little of their freedom at a time, to erode rights by a thousand tiny and almost imperceptible reductions. In this way, the people will not see those rights and freedoms being removed until past the point at which these changes cannot be reversed."*
>
> *— Adolf Hitler*

There are enough resources to sustain every person on the planet. It is because of the monopolization of resources that many people suffer around the world. It is the responsibility of the people to ensure liberty, and demand our rights when they are threatened.

> *"Earth provides enough to satisfy every man's need, but not every man's greed."*
>
> *— Mahatma Gandhi*

If we want to survive the oncoming extinction and reverse the damages that we have done to our planet, we are going to have to change the way that we perceive the world. The elite have shaped our vision of reality. We now live by the ideas and beliefs that they have created for us. To really change our situation, we are going to have to change our values and our lifestyles. We need to live in harmony with nature rather than working against it. We need to start providing for ourselves so we can take the power out of the hands of corporations.

The more we focus on the major problems of our time, the more we come to realize that they cannot be understood in isolation. They are problems that are interconnected and interdependent and must be addressed as such. For example, stabilizing the world population will only be possible when poverty is reduced worldwide. As long as there are people starving and struggling to feed their families, laws will continue to be broken and people will continue to fight each other for resources.

The problems we are experiencing are different aspects of one single crisis, which is a crisis in perception. It derives from the fact that most of us, and especially our large social institutions, subscribe to the concepts of an outdated worldview.

The reason we are faced with such a devastating situation is because humans have separated themselves from nature and the natural web of life. Our lifestyle is not in harmony with the natural world and it has affected the planet on nearly every level. We are an organism inhabiting planet Earth, we depend on the planet and its resources for our survival, as do all of Earth's inhabitants.

Human beings have the largest impact on the overall health of the planet, and therefore we should be more responsible with how we live our lives. All of the tragedies that we are experiencing today can be linked back to the actions of human beings.

If we want to survive we will have to change. We must transition from being dependent consumers to becoming responsible producers. Before I go in depth about the changes we need to make, we must first reevaluate our behavior and what it means to be a human being.

Part III

Human Behavior

Chapter 21. Reevaluating Human Nature

Throughout history, the human species has accomplished a lot. We have survived for millennia against the harsh conditions of nature and have made technological advancements that have reshaped our entire way of life. We have lived through the rise and fall of numerous civilizations, traveled to outer space beyond the boundaries of our planet, and have discovered our place in this vast Universe. Yet, when it comes to understanding the general psychological characteristics, feelings, and behavioral traits of humankind, we are almost completely clueless.

Modern man has made no significant leaps in the evolution of consciousness for thousands of years. In fact, we may even be less intelligent than some of the civilizations that have preceded us. Scientists have speculated that the gap of intelligence between great thinkers such as Einstein and Tesla compared to the average human is far greater than the gap between the average human and contemporary apes. What is it that is blocking us from achieving a superior level of intelligence?

Aside from the mental conditioning that our culture has been subjected to, I believe that it is due to an utter lack of understanding human nature. Modern humans are raised in such a negative environment. The corruption of our educational system, economic structure, and media outlets has resulted in a state of ignorance common amongst most individuals. Our society does not pay attention to our most necessary survival needs.

In order to survive, human beings need air, water, food, love, and shelter. It would make sense that we focus on the quantity and quality of each of these elements. Instead, we put social status, markets, money, and ego in front of these basic needs. As a result of our behavior, the air we breathe is polluted, the water we drink is polluted, our food is contaminated, and our ability to love is limited because we have been tricked into not loving ourselves, resulting in millions of people who are without shelter, without nourishment, and without community.

We need to understand what keeps our species alive and well. We must all focus on improving our behavior and the behavior of humans in general. It is no secret that modern man has a very violent nature. We stress, fear, hate, envy, betray, steal, manipulate, abuse, and kill far more than we relax, appreciate, admire, accept, love, give, greet, respect, and share.

Our behavior is barbaric and unacceptable. We have ignored our true nature and consequently our livelihood is mismanaged and our planet is endangered. Millions of people are suffering every day from lack of nutrition and a lack of love from their fellow human beings.

We need to reevaluate and reconsider what is appropriate human behavior. Human beings have been so successful at surviving because of our intelligence and cooperation. When we are unintelligent and uncooperative it is no wonder that our survival is threatened. We need to be educated about our health and the health of our planet, and work together to achieve goals that are impossible to achieve individually.

"We need more understanding of human nature because the only real danger that exists is man himself. He is the great danger, and we are pitifully unaware of it. We know nothing of man, far too little. His psyche should be studied, because we are the origin of all coming evil."
– Carl Gustav Jung

We fail to recognize the importance of nutrition and the health of our bodies. We need food and water to survive. Corporations have taken control of our most essential resources. They have spent billions of dollars on researching how to persuade you to purchase their products.

Processed foods are bad for our health and lack most fundamental nutrients. As a result of consumption, people have less energy and lead low vibrational lifestyles, making them easier to control. The intentional poisoning of a food supply is a form of biological warfare, and it is being used severely through governments, and the powerful corporations that influence them.

They want us to have poor nutrition because that means we will be less healthy and less aware. That is why corporations spend so much money on research and advertising; they want you to keep buying their products. We need to recognize what the corporations are doing to our food supply and how we can decrease our dependence on them.

When you eat food, there are factors that make the experience pleasurable, such as the sensation of eating the food. This includes what it tastes like, what it smells like, and how it feels in your mouth. This last quality—known as "orosensation"—can be particularly important. Food companies will spend millions of dollars to discover the most satisfying level of crunch in a potato chip. Their scientists will test for the perfect amount of fizzle in a soda. These factors all combine to create the sensation that your brain associates with a particular food or drink.[130]

Companies study what makes your brain excited and your senses stimulated so that you will want to buy more of their products. Most large

---

[130] http://jamesclear.com/junk-food-science

food companies will even add chemicals that are toxic to our bodies, as long as they stimulate our mind and convince us to keep buying their merchandise. As a result, we tend to overeat. We are eating more than our bodies can comfortably process, while still being deprived of the nutrients that real foods provide us with.

Our food industry ignores health and our health industry ignores food. Studies have shown that diet is the most effective medicine. Studies have also shown that prescription drugs are terrible for your body.[131] The majority of people seem to have no knowledge of the things that make humans healthy, and many people also show a huge lack of interest in maintaining their health.

The health of our bodies affects the health of our minds, and as many ancient religions and spiritual people have pointed out, the health of our bodies also affects the health of our spirit. Everything in the Universe is interconnected.

The health of our bodies affects the health of our minds, and the health of our minds affects the health of our society, which affects the health of our planet, and so on. We fail to recognize the intrinsic nature of everything in the Universe. We need to realize that everything connects to everything else, and what we do to one thing will dramatically affect what happens to every other thing.

---

[131] http://www.alternet.org/story/147318/100,000_americans_die_each_year_from_prescription_drugs,_while_pharma_companies_get_rich

Chapter 22. Everything Is Interconnected

"If you wish to make an apple pie from scratch you must first start with the Universe."
– Carl Sagan

This quote provides a perfect example of the interconnectedness of our Universe. It shows that even something as simple as an apple pie does not just come into existence. The apples, the flour, the cinnamon, all of the ingredients are traced back to how they were created. An apple is a product of the universe and the series of events that lead to its creation. You cannot have an apple without the events that led up to the apple. In the same way you cannot exist without the events in the Universe that created you. The Big Bang, the creation of energy and matter, dust and stars, supernovas, meteors, water, the transformation of water to life, led to the long line of hereditary genes that led to you. You are a part of the entire Universe, like a wave is a part of the entire ocean.

The piece of paper that you are reading this on is another example of how everything in the world is interconnected. This piece of paper could not exist if it was not for the clouds that provided the rain for trees to grow and become paper. Without the cloud, the rain, and the trees, there would be no paper. Something as simple as a piece of paper or a slice of apple pie shows us that nothing in the Universe can exist without everything else.

"Learn how to see. Realize that everything connects to everything else."
– Leonardo da Vinci

Understanding the connection between everything has transformed the way many deal with their own wellness—as the interconnectedness of physical, mental, emotional and spiritual health has come to be understood more and more clearly. The idea of separation, or dealing with parts individually, is actually a view introduced by the West. Eastern medical practices, health programs, and spiritual paths have long understood this reality.

Even the events in our daily lives impact everything in the Universe. It is all cause and effect. Everything is both an effect and a cause. This book is the effect of my exposure to the truth and my desire to improve the state of the world, and I am certain that it will cause some people to change their perspective on life. In return, the people affected will affect the world in a new and different way, and that will be the cause of something greater. Recognizing the connection between everything in the Universe is a great way to appreciate the beauty of life.

"Humankind has not woven the web of life. We are but one thread within it. Whatever we do to the web, we do to ourselves. All things are bound together. All things connect."

– Chief Seattle

When you do something as simple as throwing a piece of garbage out of your car window, you are changing the lives of everyone on Earth. That piece of garbage will likely be picked up by a current of wind, and be blown along the wind pattern until it reaches the ocean. Once reaching the ocean, it will flow with the ocean currents until it reaches the point where currents meet, and will be collected into an already increasing mass of garbage. Everything you do affects everything else. Every action has an equal and opposite reaction.

When we do harm to one thing we are essentially harming ourselves. For example, when we use poisonous toxins and pesticides to grow our food, we pollute the soil, kill the life of the surrounding ecosystems, and decrease the quality of the food supply, which then decreases our health and the level of energy we operate on. When we do this every day on a global scale for several decades we end up with soil infertility, habitat loss, environmental pollution, low quality food, poor health, malnutrition, and a lack of productivity, which is so apparent in today's society.

By shifting from a life lived in nature to a life in the city, human beings have changed the way that we function and have severely damaged our health. We now consume foods that bring us illness, and provide less energy, we have decreased our amount of physical exercise, and have constructed an artificial way of living life that does not take into consideration the natural environment or the physiological changes that result from a change in cultural traditions. We need to return to a more natural way of life and fast, or else we will continue to contribute to a mass extinction, one that has already begun. To do this we must change the way that we perceive the world so we can focus on what is most important.

By focusing on reality and treating everything in relation to everything else we can raise our awareness above the narrow perspective of what we experience in our daily lives, and solve our problems using a different level of thinking than the one that created them. As a society our focus should be on health, sustainability, education, and ensuring justice and liberty among all individuals. To achieve this we must inform the public of the situation we are in and encourage a positive change in our behavior. We need to evolve our consciousness and change the way that we look at the world.

"The concept of "person," like the concept of self, is made only of non-person elements - sun, clouds, wheat, space and so on. Thanks to these elements, there is something we call a person. But erecting a barrier between the idea of person and the idea of non-person is erroneous. If we say, for example, animals, plants, the moon, the stars, and so forth, exist to serve us, we are caught up in the idea of a person. These kinds of concepts are used to separate self from nonself and person from non-person, and they are erroneous.

We put a lot of energy into advancing technology in order to serve our lives better, and we exploit the non-human elements, such as the forests, rivers, and oceans, in order to do so. But as we pollute and destroy nature, we pollute and destroy ourselves as well. The results of discriminating between human and non-human are global warming, pollution, and the emergence of many strange diseases. In order to protect ourselves, we must protect the non-human elements. This fundamental understanding is needed if we want to protect our planet and ourselves."

-Thich Nhat Hanh

Our health is dependent upon the health of where we live—in the large scope, Earth, and in the narrow scope, our homes and work places. And this is true on all levels. If you are eating foods that are not nutritious, and you are drinking water with poisons in it, your health and potential will be greatly limited. If you work in a place where the culture is negative, your spirit will be depleted, which will cause your energy and health to decline. The examples are limitless.

Everything is connected. How you live your life affects all other life. Consider the Butterfly Effect: What you do will dramatically effect what happens next. Put yourself in good environments. Help create good environments. Be a positive influence—it is all connected.

"When we try to pick out anything by itself, we find it hitched to everything else in the universe."

– John Muir

Chapter 23. Similarities Between Humans

Many of us act like we are so different from one another; maybe it is because of our skin color, our body type, the language we speak, or the personality we have, but in reality we are essentially all the same.

Physically, all humans are born with relatively the same body structure. We all have bones, skin, a heart, a brain, a head, a torso, etc. Even though some people may be born with defects or do not have certain body parts, we are fundamentally the same. We all breathe air and bleed blood, our skin color is only different due to the geographic location of our ancestors, and all of us can be traced back to the same rudimentary organisms.

Even animals share many of the same qualities that we do. Aside from some physical similarities, all beings are conscious and have their own conscious experience. All living things have similar goals of obtaining nourishment, seeking companionship and avoiding pain. Yet, even though these traits are easily recognizable, there are more than 150 billion animals slaughtered worldwide every year, which is an average of more than 4,000 per second.[132]

Sentient beings with emotions like you and me are tortured, beaten, and slaughtered every single second of the day. All to provide us with food that we do not even necessarily need to eat for survival. Not only is this tragic in regard to animal life, but it has serious repercussions for our environment, and it shows us truly just how much empathy our species

[132] http://www.adaptt.org/killcounter.html

lacks. We need to see the similarities between all living things and treat them respectfully.

"The idea that some lives matter less is the root of all that is wrong with the world."
– Paul Farmer, American physician and anthropologist, and founder of Partners in Health

The biggest difference between humans is the way that we think. Everyone has a different thought process, but the way we achieve this thought process is the same. We all think the way that we do due to our environmental influences. A child is born with a blank state of mind. As they observe the things around them, they develop different traits and characteristics. You are the same way. You are the way that you are because it was how you were raised by your culture, but when you were born your mind was a blank canvas of consciousness just like everyone else's.

Some people are less fortunate than others, and have to be raised in negative environments. As a result, they may have a negative mindset, but deep down they are really the same. We all experience life based on our surroundings and we all experience the same emotions. Realizing the similarity between everyone is a great way to improve the well being of the human family. Look at your neighbors with eyes of compassion; try to see the world through their eyes before you judge them.

Chapter 24. Similarities Between Religions

Another similarity many of us do not recognize is the similarity between religions. There is actually a field of study that investigates these similarities called comparative religion. Comparative religion is defined as: the branch of the study of religions concerned with the systematic comparison of the doctrines and practices of the world's religions.

A lot of people blindly accept their religion without considering other possibilities. I would like to apologize ahead of time if I offend anyone with what I am about to say; that is not my intention. I realize that religion is often a touchy subject, so I will try to choose my words carefully. I am not trying to disrespect any religion, but do you believe in its practice, or do you believe in it because the majority of people you know believe it as well? Have you considered that your beliefs could just be based on your geographic location or the way you were raised?

Every religion is just a different interpretation of nature, but many people have strong beliefs in a religion they seem to know nothing about. If this applies to you, stop and think for a moment. Do you really believe what you have been taught, or have you just accepted an opinion that the majority of people around you share? Do you think your religion is the truth, or do you fear that if it is the truth and you do not believe it, that you will be punished in the afterlife?

"If people are only good because they
fear punishment and hope for reward, then
we are a sorry lot indeed."

– Albert Einstein

I can tell you right now that what we refer to as God is not the "man in the sky" character that most Christians believe. There is no possible way that a deity could govern and observe in detail every single fraction of the universe. What we refer to as God is something that is inside of all of us, it is the essence of our being—the energy of the universe, our natural state of consciousness.

Many Christians believe in a god that is outside of them, the "man in the sky" character – but Jesus himself even said, "The kingdom of God is within you" (Luke 17:21). This inner kingdom of god has had many names. Plato refers to it as the Good and the Beautiful, Aristotle as Being, Plotinus as the Infinite, Hindus refer to it as Akasha, St. Bernard as the Word, Ralph Waldo Emerson as the Oversoul. In Taoism it is called the Tao, in Judaism Ein Sof. Among Australian aboriginals it is called the dream time. The names may differ, but the inner reality that they point to is one and the same. God is within you and can be directly experienced by you. You do not have to search outward for God. Look into every great religious, spiritual, and wisdom tradition and we find the same precept: that life's ultimate truth, its ultimate treasure, lies within.

> *"I believe in God, but not as one thing, not as an old man in the sky. I believe that what people call God is something in all of us. I believe that what Jesus, and Mohammed, and Buddha and all the rest said was right. It's just that the translations have gone wrong."*
>
> *– John Lennon*

Religion is a human attempt to understand the complexity of nature, but nature cannot be fully understood by human intellect, which is why most religions require blind faith to make up for a lack of evidence. The reason it is impossible to know the true reality of nature is because that which is perceived to be nature is only the idea of nature aspiring in each person's mind. When we give names to things, we isolate them from nature and nature is not seen in its true form. An object seen in isolation from the whole is not the real thing.

"Once you label me, you negate me."
– Soren Kierkegaard

To see nature in its true form we must eliminate all of the things that we use to define nature, and experience the present moment. We have to see the world as an infant does. Infants see the world clearly without thinking, having no fixed definition of what it is they are experiencing. To see the world as an infant does we must return to our natural minds.

The purpose of many spiritual practices, such as meditation, is to silence the mind and directly experience our natural state of awareness. We spend the majority of our lives constantly thinking one thought or another. Hardly ever do we simply sit and experience life without being fixated on our thoughts. Instead of just being happy, we think about what it feels like to be happy, ruining the experience. We do this much more often than we realize.

The reason we do this is because we have formed an image of ourselves, what is commonly referred to as an "ego." The purpose of this is so that we can get a sense of who we are and what our relationship is with our environment. The function of the ego is to identify oneself with the physical world.

Unfortunately, we tend to get fixated on the idea of us and so we act in a way that makes our ego seem more important. We buy certain clothes, say certain things, and act in a certain way so that we can fit in and impress others. This need for attention is a function of the ego to ensure its existence in the world—though we are not our egos, and we will exist regardless of whether or not we choose to abide by our self-constructed identities.

You, experiencing life right now, the person who is reading these words, this state of awareness—this is your conscious mind, and it is completely separate from your ego. The reason we tend to ignore this is because we allow our egos to interfere with our conscious mind. Realizing that we are not our idea of ourselves requires us to see our existence objectively, which leads to the destruction of the ego.

When your ego feels threatened your natural “fight-or-flight” response kicks in. This is a primitive function of our brain’s central core, which causes us to avoid anything that threatens our survival. When our beliefs are challenged we tend to dismiss certain information if it does not enforce our idea of the world. In psychology this is known as cognitive dissonance.

Cognitive dissonance refers to a situation involving conflicting attitudes, beliefs or behaviors. This situation produces a feeling of discomfort leading to an alteration in one of the attitudes, beliefs, or behaviors to reduce the discomfort and restore balance.[133] When a person is given new information that challenges their beliefs, they will likely refuse to accept the information as true, in order to avoid feeling discomfort. This habit of rejecting new information is limiting our potential. If we want to

---

[133] http://www.simplypsychology.org/cognitive-dissonance.html

evolve as a species, it is critical that we learn to adapt to new information, even when it goes against everything that we believe.

> *"The ultimate ignorance is the rejection of something you know nothing about, yet refuse to investigate."*
> *– Dr. Wayne Dyer*

Our ego is a tool to help us survive and make sense of the outside world. It gives us the ability to understand what is good for our physical well-being and what is not. Its purpose is to ensure the perseverance of the individual. When we think that our ego is who we really are as sentient beings, we begin to lose our connection with the natural world, focusing only on what is beneficial to our survival and not the survival of the planet as a whole. To see past the confines of the ego, we must become more in tune with our hearts and our natural mind, our direct experience of consciousness.

Try to sit quietly in a peaceful environment, close your eyes, allow the breath to flow naturally, breathing deeply, and see if you can directly experience awareness. Watch your thoughts as they come and go. Realize that you are not your thoughts.

Our mind is like a tape player that never stops, constantly producing thoughts in our heads. Meditation allows us to create a space between ourselves and our thoughts, giving us a sense of our true being. It allows us to be calm and centered, without being controlled by our thoughts and emotions. When we waste our time overthinking we ruin our life experience. We do this because we do not realize who we really are. We use our self-constructed egos to define us, not the substance of our being.

To get more in-tune with your true self, your natural subconscious mind, you need to silence your mind often and directly experience the awareness that is you. This is the purpose of meditation.

Silence the mind and cultivate awareness.

Our society is very brain-dominant; we view the brain as the center of our being. We have forgotten how to listen to our heart. As a result, we have become very headstrong. Our heart has its own unique intelligence that we must reacquaint ourselves with.

Our heart is more than just an organ that pumps life-giving oxygenated and nutrient-rich blood throughout our bodies. Now, researchers are learning that this marvelous machine, the size of a fist and weighing on average less than 10 ounces, also possesses a level of intelligence they are only beginning to understand. Evidence shows the heart also plays a greater role in our mental, emotional, and physical processes than previously thought.

The heart, like the brain, generates a powerful electromagnetic field.[134] The heart generates the largest electromagnetic field in the body. The electrical field as measured in an electrocardiogram (ECG) is about 60 times greater in amplitude than the brain waves recorded in an electroencephalogram (EEG). The heart's electromagnetic field contains certain information or coding that is transmitted throughout and outside of the body. One of the most significant findings related to this field is that intentionally generated positive emotions can change this information or coding.

---

[134] https://www.heartmath.org/articles-of-the-heart/science-of-the-heart/the-energetic-heart-is-unfolding/

Every living thing produces an electromagnetic field. Our heart produces an electromagnetic field that changes with our emotions. When you are fearful, angry, upset, anxious, depressed, or feeling negative emotions, your electromagnetic field disrupts your immune system. If you are loving, happy, grateful, or feeling other positive emotions, your heart's electromagnetic field is in its best condition. Your emotions have a severe impact on the way that your physical body performs.

Our heart rate reflects the number of heartbeats that take place in a given minute. The way that you breathe determines the speed at which your heart beats and thus the vibrational frequency of its electromagnetic field. Whenever we are confronted with potential dangers (e.g., walking alone at night, being chased by a wild animal), we enact a fight-or-flight response in which our heart rate spikes up, our breathing gets shallower, our muscles tense up, and so on. The *sympathetic* branch of the nervous system mediates this response, which is essential for survival.[135]

When we maintain deep, slow, and relaxed abdominal breathing, our heart rate is also relaxed, thus so is our vibrational frequency and the vibrational frequency of the things around us. Your energy is like a magnet; you attract to you whatever vibration you send out. Unaware of this law, people will tune to your frequency just as you can unknowingly allow yourself to tune to theirs. Being aware of this process can bring about great things in your life. However, ignorance of it can result in much harm to your physical and mental health.

Electricity, defined by Merriam-Webster, is: "a fundamental form of energy observable in positive and negative forms that occurs naturally (as

---

[135] http://www.sciencedaily.com/terms/sympathetic_nervous_system.htm

in lightning) or is produced (as in a generator) and that is expressed in terms of the movement and interaction of electrons."

Usually, when thinking of electricity, we think of it as something external to our bodies. However, there is a form of electricity that is prevalent in every living creature: bioelectricity.

Bioelectromagnetics, also known as bioelectromagnetism, is the study of the interaction between electromagnetic fields and biological entities. Within all living organisms there are electric potentials and currents, some that are self-produced and others that are results of environmental energies. The electric phenomenon of living organisms is known as bioelectricity.

Bioelectricity is what allows a shark to chart the ocean floor. It is bioelectromagnetic phenomena that allow birds and whales to migrate great distances at the same time each year with great accuracy. It is bioelectricity that enables the electric eel to produce a current of nearly 1,000 volts.

The human body runs largely off of bioelectricity and has organs dedicated to sensing electromagnetic impulses, both inside and outside of the body. The pineal and pituitary glands are both directly tied to the human body's ability to sense and actively experience electromagnetic phenomenon.[136]

The nervous system in human beings is based entirely off of the ability to transmit electric pulses. Every cell within the human body pumps ions in and out of the cell for energy purposes; known as the sodium-potassium pump, and is found in all living organisms.

---

[136] http://www.chienergyheals.com/bioelectricity-qi-and-the-human-body/

Qi or chi (pronounced *chee*) is a term for these electromagnetic phenomena. For hundreds of years, the Chinese have been aware of the electromagnetic energy generated by human beings, and use this knowledge to maintain health and prevent disease. Their traditional method of cultivating Qi energy is known as Qigong or Chi Kung. The Chinese have recently used this method in conjunction with modern medicine to cure cancer, immune system disorders, and other life-threatening conditions.

The cosmos has certain types of wave energy, and all living things have their own unique wave energies. When an organism's wave energies have been damaged by environmental stimuli and stress, the cells in its body send out a signal called dis-ease. The Chinese have realized that they can heal the wave energies of organisms, thus eliminating dis-ease in the body.

The same phenomenon is also recognized in Hinduism; its name for it is Prana. Prana is a Sanskrit word literally meaning 'life-force,' the invisible bioenergy that keeps the body alive and maintains a state of good health. In Hinduism, Prana is the infinite energy from which matter is born, also interpreted as the vital, life-sustaining force of both the individual body and the Universe.

Our life force bioenergy has been known by a multitude of names around the world. For instance: Ki is the Japanese equivalent of chi or life energy; Lung is a Tibetan word meaning inner 'winds' of life force; Ruach Ha Kodesh is Hebrew for Breath of God; Nafs and Ruh is the Islamic terms for a kind of 'soul breath'; Spiritus Sancti is the Latin (Catholic) term meaning 'Holy Spirit'; Pneuma is Greek for 'vital breath'; Élan vital is the term for 'vital life-force' in classical European Vitalism; Orgone was the revolutionary psycho-biologist Wilhelm Reich's term for vital life force;

nilch'i is the Navajo term for 'sacred life-giving wind or life-force'; ni is the Lakota Sioux term for life-force; Mana is an Oceanic-Polynesian term (and more recently also adopted as the term for life-force by several fantasy role-playing games); ha, or the more-specifically Hawaiian (Huna), is the term for 'breath' or sacred life force; Ka is the Ancient Egyptian idea of a vital essence or life energy; and, of course, the classic term for bio-energy that George Lucas adopted for his modern classic *Star Wars* is 'the Force.'

Many different religions share common beliefs, but just have different ways of explaining their beliefs. As long as a religion promotes equality, peace, freedom, love, and health, then there should be nothing wrong with what religion someone chooses to practice.

When people refer to God, they are actually referring to nature, our vital life-force energy and the natural source of consciousness within us, although most are unaware of this. It is understandable that man created religion to try to explain this natural phenomenon, but as we broaden our understanding of the Universe, we need to realize when it is necessary to let go of our beliefs and adapt to new information.

Many people argue over who follows the right religion, without knowing the history of their own religion. Many followers of religion are so strung up in their beliefs that they refuse to have an open mind towards any other possibility. Would you honestly want to live a lie your whole life because you are too afraid to accept the truth? The problem with religion is that it teaches people to be satisfied with not understanding. We need to see past the dogma of religion and heal the relationship between our planet and ourselves.

We must stop confusing religion and spirituality. Religion is a set of rules, regulations and rituals created by humans, which was suppose to help people grow spiritually. Due to human imperfection religion has become corrupt, political, divisive and a tool for power struggle. Spirituality is not theology or ideology. It is simply a way of life, pure and original as was given by the Most High of Creation. Spirituality is a network linking us to the Most High, the universe, and each other..."

— Haile Selassie I

There is no way to know for sure whether a deity like God exists, or whether we will be aware of our existence after death. These things are beyond the ability of people to know. We do not know what happens to our consciousness after we die, because we have not died yet.

Rather than focusing on our future, we should do our best to improve our lives now, in the present moment. We know that we are humans, we know what our bodies require for good health, we know what is good and what is bad for the environment, we know the difference between right and wrong, so why do we continue to live in suffering?

The truth is that many people actually do not know the basics to human life, and that is precisely what is wrong with the world. The information is out there but it has been hidden from us, and that is the reason that I have written this book, to inform *YOU*. For our entire lives we have been told how and what to think by people who simply do not know. The destiny of each person lies with each person. It is up to the individual to determine what they believe, and it is up to the culture to ensure that the environment people are raised in is both peaceful and healthy.

We must respect the religious and philosophical beliefs of each individual, as we all have an individual experience, yet we must also strive for an understanding of truth based on logic and factual evidence. We must also understand that we have an incomplete understanding of the universe, and that there are certain things we are just not capable of comprehending with our limited sensory perception. Above all, we must recognize what is healthy for humans, animals, trees, and the planet as a whole, for all have an effect on one another. Humans have the largest impact on the health of the planet; therefore, it is our responsibility to ensure that the planet and all that inhabit it remain in a state of optimal health.

> *"The religion of the future will be a cosmic religion. It will have to transcend a personal God and avoid dogma and theology. Encompassing both the natural and the spiritual, it will have to be based on a religious sense arising from the experience of all things, natural and spiritual, considered as a meaningful unity."*
> *– Albert Einstein*

We need to return to ourselves and to our connection with each other and the world around us. Being a human being, in the sense of being born to the human species, must be defined also in terms of becoming a human being. A baby is only potentially a human being, and must grow into humanness in the society, the culture, and the family. Many of us today are still growing into the stage of becoming a human being. It is important that we keep that in mind when speaking to those who are less informed, that there was a time when we did not know what we know today.

Many people are completely unaware of the things I have covered in this book, but it is important that we lead humanity in the direction of peace, love, understanding, justice, and truth. Many people are closed minded and not willing to accept the truth. As a part of the human family, we need to be willing to adjust to people's understanding, and inform them based on their willingness to learn. This can only be achieved with compassion. When we begin to see everyone else as a part of ourselves, when we can step into someone's shoes and see the world from their perspective, we will be able to properly guide our culture to one that is more peaceful and loving. Ultimately, we need to enlighten the people to the situation that our society is in, and the threat we are posing to our environment. If we remain ignorant, we will not survive much longer.

> *"When we look at modern man, we have to face the fact that modern man suffers from a kind of poverty of the spirit, which stands in glaring contrast with a scientific and technological abundance. We have learned to fly the air as birds, we've learned to swim the seas as fish, yet we haven't learned to walk the Earth as brothers and sisters."*
>
> *– Martin Luther King Jr.*

Chapter 25. Returning To Our True Selves

As individuals, it is important that we recognize who we are at our deepest level of existence. Many people live their lives trying to avoid their true self, buying expensive clothes, or listening to popular music to fit in. We need to realize that material things will not bring us happiness. Nothing outside of ourselves will bring us happiness. If your happiness is dependent upon objects or the opinions of others, then your happiness can be taken away. We need to learn to be happy for no reason. Being happy and living a positive life will improve our well-being.

One of the reasons so many people suffer is because they are too attached to the physical world. In order for there to be attachment, you need two things—the person or thing being attached to, and the person who's attaching. In other words, "attachment" requires self-reference, and it requires seeing the object of attachment as separate from oneself. Seeing oneself and everything else in this way is a delusion. Further, it is a delusion that is the deepest cause of our unhappiness. It is because we mistakenly see ourselves as separate from everything else to which we "attach."

Because we think we have intrinsic existence within our skin, and what's outside our skin is "everything else," we go through life grabbing for one thing after another to make us feel safe, or to make us happy. We "pursue" happiness because we think it comes from outside of ourselves. But it's also because we think things are outside of ourselves that we are stressed about them and worry about them. The more that you are attached to the physical world, the harder it will be for you to let go when you die. Learning to detach ourselves from our beliefs will prevent much anger and stress. We need to realize the interconnectedness of all things, and accept that we are a part of everything in the Universe.

> *"A human being is a part of the whole called by us universe, a part limited in time and space. He experiences himself, his thoughts and feelings as something separated from the rest, a kind of optical delusion of his consciousness. This delusion is a kind of prison for us, restricting us to our personal desires and to affection for a few persons nearest to us. Our task must be to free ourselves from this prison by widening our circle of compassion to embrace all living creatures and the whole of nature in its beauty."*
>
> *– Albert Einstein*

The true nature of self is non-self. A human being cannot exist without non-human elements. The air, water, earth, sun—all of these things are necessary for us to exist. We are afraid of death because ignorance gives us an illusory perception of what death is. In reality, nothing is born and nothing dies.

When you look at this piece of paper, you think that there was a moment in time when it came into existence, a moment in the factory it became a piece of paper. But before it was a sheet of paper, was it nothing? Did its existence come from nothing? Before it was a sheet of paper, it must have been something else—a tree, a branch, sunshine, clouds, the Earth. If you were to burn the paper right now would it cease to exist? If the paper were burned it would turn into smoke, heat and ash—it would continue to exist in a different form. Just like the piece of paper, you were never really born and you will never really die; your existence will continue to live on.

Everything is connected and nothing has an independent existence. Looking at things in this way will relieve a lot of our suffering. We often suffer because we are too attached to the concepts of our lives and ourselves. When these things begin to change, as everything inevitably does, we suffer because we cling to the idea of them being permanent.

Another thing that many people are too attached to is their relationships with others. Relationships are a beautiful thing, and it is important that we learn to love all living things, but many people get too attached to others and allow the thought of them to consume their being. This causes people to depend on others for their happiness rather than making themselves happy. Often people will also become so attached to their circle of friends that they block out other people from entering their lives. As a result, many people lead superficial lives, only focusing on what directly affects them and the people they are close to.

All people are unique, yet essentially the same at a fundamental level. As humans, we need to love everyone, not just the people that we have gotten to know. Every person is part of the extended human family. Getting too attached to certain people will result in suffering. To avoid this suffering, we need to treat all people like they are family, appreciate when they are in our lives, and understand that they will not always be there.

Death

Death is a great way to recognize impermanence and interconnectedness. We are all going to die one day, but who among us really believes it? It is an obvious fact yet so many of us pretend like it will never happen. Death is life's greatest teacher. We should all keep the reality of death in the forefront of our consciousness so we can better prioritize our daily activities, and direct our attention to that which is most significant and meaningful. It is important that we accept death before we die. Understanding that nothing is permanent helps us appreciate what exists in the present moment.

Death is nothing to fear. Everything dies: planets, solar systems, galaxies, animals, people—all are impermanent. Death is a part of life. For instance, soil is created when living organisms die and their carcasses mix with the matrix of clay, sand, and gravel. Without the death of organisms creating soil, we would have no substance for growing plant life, and would have no food for our survival. Without the death of stars creating many of the elements in the Universe, we would not exist today. These are just a few of many examples providing the need for death in order to sustain life.

It is hard for us to comprehend the differences that things make when they appear to have little effect on our daily lives; but nature is cyclical and everything is interconnected. Death is a part of life. It supports the possibility of life and to wish for eternal life is selfish. We must learn to give and receive in order to maintain such a perfect balance. Be grateful that you are given a chance to experience life, and when it comes time to pass on, do not be afraid. Death gives birth to life and we must allow others to share the experience.

Though our physical body will deteriorate, our energy will continue to live on. The first law of thermodynamics is that energy cannot be created or destroyed, it can only be transferred. Every inch of your body is abundant with energy. When you die, this energy will not be destroyed, it must be transferred to another source. Your vibrational energy attracts things of similar frequencies. When you die, your vibrational energy will likely be transferred to something of a similar frequency, a process that Buddhists view as reincarnation.

"All one's thoughts, words and deeds, both good and bad, are imprinted on one's mind, and after the disintegration of the physical body at death, one's mental vibrations will attract appropriate subatomic particles and forces for rebirth at an appropriate place according to the karmic effect of those vibrations."

– Wong Kiew Kit

Whether reincarnation is an actual fact is hard to say, but the science behind it is convincing. Our energy must go somewhere, wherever it ends up will essentially be a form of rebirth. Regardless of your views on death, our existence will live on in some form or another, whether physically, spiritually, or socially. Even if we were to completely cease to exist at the point of death, the ways in which our lives affected the world will continue to echo throughout eternity. Our fear of death is just a fear of the unknown. Death is every living thing's final destination, so there is no need for us to stress over the possibility of death; it is inevitable. Our unnecessary fears of death only disturb our experience of life in the present moment.

"Each separate being in the universe returns to the common source. Returning to the source is serenity. If you don't realize the source, you stumble in confusion and sorrow. When you realize where you come from, you naturally become tolerant, disinterested, amused, kindhearted as a grandmother, dignified as a king. Immersed in the wonder of the Tao, you can deal with whatever life brings you, and when death comes, you are ready."

– Lao Tzu

Desire

Another reason that many people suffer is because of their desires. The word "greed" usually is defined as attempting to possess more than one needs or deserves, especially at the expense of others. We're taught from childhood that we shouldn't be greedy. To "desire," however, is simply to want something very much. Our culture doesn't attach a moral judgment to desire. A desire for material possessions is encouraged, and not just through advertising. People who have earned wealth and the possessions that go with it are held up as role models.

Like attachments, we allow our desires to consume us. For example, if we see a pair of shoes we think we must have, even though we have a closet full of perfectly good shoes, we feel that we need them in order to be happy. As strange as it seems, we do this more often than most people notice.

Because our culture implicitly values desire, we are unprepared for its dangers. At this very moment, the world is reeling from a financial meltdown, and entire industries are on the edge of collapse. The crisis has many causes, but a big one is that many people made many very bad decisions because they became greedy. Our culture looks up to moneymakers—and moneymakers believe themselves to be wise and honorable. Because of this, we don't see the destructive force of desire until it is too late.

Much of the world's economy is fueled by desire and consumption. Because people buy things, things must be manufactured and marketed, which gives people jobs so they have money to buy things. If people stop buying things, there is less demand, and people are laid off from their jobs.

Corporations that make consumer goods spend fortunes developing new products and persuading consumers through advertising that they must have these new products. Thus greed grows the economy, but as we see from the financial crisis, greed also can destroy it.

We need to learn how to be content with what we have. When it comes to purchasing things from businesses and corporations, we must learn to distinguish between the wholesome and the unwholesome—what supports our well-being and what hinders it.

To be content with what we have starts with appreciation and gratitude. Be grateful for everything you have in your life: food, water, shelter, family, air, trees, vision, a functional body, and everything else. Some people do not appreciate what they have until it is gone.

When we are grateful for what we have and show appreciation, we are overwhelmed with a sense of joy and wholeness. To be content with what you have, is to live gracefully among the Earth. To be content with everything you have is important, but what is more important is to be content with yourself.

Transforming Suffering into Peace

"Don't take anything personally, nothing others do is because of you. What others say and do is a projection of their own reality, their own dream. When you are immune to the opinions of others, you won't be the victim of needless suffering."

– Don Miguel Ruiz

Many people do not accept themselves. They live in fear, doubt, anxiety, insecurity, and let their lives reflect a negative mindset. We need to learn to accept ourselves, for no one will accept you until you learn to accept yourself. We can do this by not comparing ourselves to others, and by taking pride in the things that we do. If we do things for a good cause, then we feel good about ourselves. People will continue to disrespect others and try to bring them down because they are jealous. Jealousy is a primitive emotion. Those who are jealous are usually still living in a negative and narrow state of mind. We should want what is best for our friends and neighbors, not envy them for what they have.

We tend to let our emotions lead our life, and as a result we are left with much pain and unwholesome feelings. Some would argue that most of our physical, mental and relational problems come from our inability to adequately experience emotions. We deny, bury, project, rationalize, medicate, drink away, smother in comfort food, sleep off, sweat out, and sweep under the rug our sadness, anger, and fear. Some people spend more energy on avoiding their emotions than others do on actually feeling them. Give yourself unconditional permission to feel your feelings. When you feel safe enough to let your guard down, whether that's alone or with someone you trust, you can focus on the situation, fully experience the feelings and may then be able to better understand why it hurts and what you want to do about the situation. When you can sit back and observe your emotions instead of allowing them to control you, you can learn how to better experience life.

Many of us have emotional habits that we follow unknowingly. Like getting angry over competition, fearing new things, being anxious in public, or being insecure of who we are. We need to transform our negative habits into positive habits.

Your mind is like a garden, and your thoughts are like seeds. When you have good thoughts, they become thought patterns, and result in positive habitual thinking. When you have negative thoughts, they become thought patterns, and result in negative habitual thinking. Your thoughts affect your life. When you have a good thought you are planting a good seed in your subconscious mind. If nurtured properly, this seed will grow into a flower of positive thought patterns. Your life will be positive because the way that you perceive life is positive. The same goes for if you plant negative seeds in your subconscious.

It may appear that thinking something negative may have little to no effect on your life, but when you have these thoughts, you are planting seeds in your subconscious. The seeds will continue to grow until you always think negatively, and when you do so, your life will be negative in return. It is important to always be aware of the thoughts that you have. Are they improving your life? Or are they slowly destroying it? The choice is up to you whether you decide to be an optimistic and positive thinker, or a pessimistic and negative thinker. Regardless, the thoughts that you have will affect your subconscious mind more than they will affect your conscious mind.

The thoughts that we have control our life. We need to liberate ourselves from the negative thought patterns many of us are stuck in. Such as judging others, doubting ourselves, being lazy, having no ambition—these mindsets will result in much suffering if we allow them to continue.

We are made up of our physical form, our senses, our perceptions, our habits, our prejudices, our consciousness and our awareness. These things govern our lives. If we want to have control over our lives, we need to have control over these combinations that are our existence.

"The mind is a powerful force. It can enslave us or empower us. It can plunge us into the depths of misery or take us to the heights of ecstasy. Learn to use the power wisely."

– David Cushieri

When we live a positive life, one that benefits our health, our self, our environment, and the people around us, we are setting in motion a great momentum of good karma. As I said earlier, everything is both the cause and effect of everything else. Everything you do is either helping or harming humanity.

Living the negative lifestyle that we have led for centuries is taking a toll on the Earth. More than half of the world's forests have been cut down, and as a result the planet's ecosystems are disappearing. Over 3 million acres of forest have been cut down since 1947.[137]

In the past 100 years, half of the species that lived on Earth have died. Around the turn of the 20th century, there were 30 million different species of life on Earth. In 1993, there were about 15 million. It took billions of years to create these life forms, and in less than a blink of an eye, a mere hundred years, half of the life on Earth is dead. If you were to observe this planet from space it would appear to be dying very, very rapidly. Yet we're going on as though nothing is happening and everything is under control. Yet, from an honest point of view, we have a real life and death situation here on Earth, and very few people seem to be aware of it.

When we destroy nature, we do not realize that we are destroying ourselves. Did anyone ever stop to think what would happen when every tree has been cut down, and all of our resources have been polluted? Every day we have the choice to either help or harm nature, and this choice originates from the nature within us. When you see the world, do you look with eyes of compassion, recognizing the connection between everything? Or do you see everything as separate from yourself? The "me against the world" attitude is resulting in a hurt society with no sense of community.

We all decide how we live our lives. Our actions determine our lifestyle; it is important that you pay attention to the little things you do throughout

[137] http://www.livescience.com/27692-deforestation.html

the day. If you have a habit of throwing garbage out of your car window, or destroying plant-life, or any other harmful and negative habits, then you are part of the problem, and you need to take responsibility in changing those habits. We are all responsible for the condition of the world. Making the right choices, to make this a better place to live, is your decision.

The small things that we do add up and have a large impact. The part is what makes the whole, like a piece of pie makes up the whole pie. In the same way, microorganisms make up macroorganisms.

When the cells in our body are damaged, it results in the damage of the rest of our body. Similarly, when our minds and daily habits are damaged, it results in the damage of the Earth.

Earth is one large ecosystem that is made up of many smaller ecosystems. When we damage the small ecosystems little by little, it affects the Earth on a large scale. Polluting a pond pollutes the fish in that pond, the polluted fish in the pond pollute the birds that feed on the fish, and the polluted birds pollute their predators and so on. When we cut down a forest, it destroys the ecosystem and the life that depends on that ecosystem.

We cannot provide artificial ecosystems and expect animals to thrive. They need a natural habitat, just like we do. We depend on our habitat, and the animals within that habitat for our survival. If we do not return to a more natural way of life, and fast, we have no choice but to face a mass extinction, a risk that is already rapidly increasing.

Chapter 26. Learning to Love

"An individual has not started living until he can rise above the narrow confines of his individualistic concerns to the broader concerns of all humanity."
– Martin Luther King, Jr.

The most powerful force in the universe is love. Love is what unites everything together. Every thought, word, and action is driven by a feeling based on either love or fear, so naturally we should learn to overcome fear and become more loving if we want a better life experience. Many have been taught that to have love requires having someone else love you. This just leads people to restrict the amount of love they feel based on how much others love them. You cannot measure love. It originates within us and it is infinite.

Love is as essential to us as air, a force that drives us all. It determines who we are, who we become, what we can achieve, and through this, how the world will evolve. It doesn't matter how much your parents did or didn't love you, how many friends you have or don't have, or whether your partner does or doesn't express their love to you. Only you allow or stop the flow of love into your life.

Without love there is nothing that binds us together. We live in a vast Universe where there is no sign of life for millions of light years. For small beings such as us, the immensity of the Universe is only bearable through love. Everything that we love about life we have experienced on this small rock in an infinite sea of space.

Earth is all that we have. We need to protect it. We can do this by bringing an end to mass pollution, deforestation, and industrialization. How we bring an end to these dangers is by informing those that are ignorant to the situation, and making the people more aware of their power to create change. This is only achievable through love. Love is the force that drives us to improve the planet. It is out of the love for our fellow human beings, animals, trees, oceans, and life that we strive to make this a better place to live.

By embracing our negative habits with love, we can move humanity in the direction of peace. We will not create a better Earth by separating ourselves with borders, fighting each other in wars, and arguing over our ideals. We need to walk the streets expressing love in everything we do. Appreciate life, show compassion for all living things, help each other out, form a community, be kind to strangers, be open, and listen to one another. That is how you express love. Not by violence, arguments, greed, power, competition, negative conversation, and condescending lifestyles.

When we learn to love one another, we will recognize the things that benefit humanity as a whole, rather than what benefits our selfish behavior as individuals. To do this, we need to understand our oneness with the universe. We all came from the same source and we will all return to the same source. Every one of us is an intrinsic part of our environment, and we each need to begin acting in a way that respects life and the natural world.

"Love and compassion are necessities, not luxuries.
Without them humanity cannot survive."
– Dalai Lama

By loving each other and the world we live in, we can work together toward the common goal of peace. When people work together toward a common goal, they are unstoppable. We need to be willing to work toward a positive goal. Instead of "fighting" the negatives, we need to collaborate on creating and enhancing the positives. Elevating the economic power of all people, living in peace in mutually beneficial ways, and respecting the religious beliefs of others even if they are different than ours, as long as they have positive impacts on the living.

"Never doubt that a small group of thoughtful, committed, citizens can change the world. Indeed, it is the only thing that ever has."

– Margaret Mead

We must see the big picture. There are bigger things going on than the events that you experience in your daily life. We cannot get caught up in irrelevant distractions put out by the media. If we decide to work together toward the common goal of peace, then we cannot be stopped.

"We need tremendous energy to bring about a psychological change in ourselves as human beings, because we have lived far too long in a world of make-belief, in a world of brutality, violence, despair, anxiety. To live humanly, sanely, one has to change. To bring about a change within oneself and therefore within society, one needs this radical energy, for the individual is not different from society — the society is the individual and the individual is the society. And to bring about a necessary radical, essential change in the structure of society — which is corrupt, which is immoral — there must be change in the human heart and mind."

– Jiddu Krishnamurti

Part IV
The Solution

Chapter 27. Time to Evolve

"Folks, it's time to evolve. That's why we're troubled. You know why our institutions are failing us, the church, the state, everything is failing? It's because they're no longer relevant. We're supposed to keep evolving. Evolution did not end with us growing opposable thumbs. You do know that, right?"
– Bill Hicks

Talking about peace is not enough. Each of us individually needs to live a lifestyle that promotes peace, good will, and love in everything that we do. Actions speak louder than words. If you do not actually live a life that benefits the Earth and its inhabitants, then you are part of the reason why our planet is dying. We cannot fight negative with negative; we need to start living a positive life. This is more than just a saying. Living positively sets in motion a force with great momentum. The more people that embody this force, the stronger it becomes.

Just because the only stories covered on the news are negative and fear-based, does not mean that there is not love and positivity at work. Revolutions are happening around the globe. People are standing up to the corruption of their governments and demanding their rights. It has happened throughout history and it is currently happening in Egypt, the Middle East, United States, Brazil, Africa, Turkey, Venezuela, Ukraine and many other places. This is the beginning of a global revolution.

"The planet is being destroyed. We are creating an underclass and exploiting poor people all over the world. And the legitimate problems of the people are not being addressed by our political power."
- Russell Brand

A global revolution is the last thing that the rich people in power want to happen, so of course it is not documented on any major media outlet. Regardless of what the media says, the people are waking up to the truth and the potential is incredible. What we do with this potential and how we choose to guide it is extremely important.

Chapter 28. Resource-Based Economy

There are many ways that we can take action in creating a better life here on Earth. One of the ways is by shifting from a monetary society based on debt to a resource-based economy. The following excerpt is cited from the Venus Project website[138], founded by Jacque Fresco, the person who originated the idea of a resource-based economy.

> *"The term and meaning of a Resource Based Economy was originated by Jacque Fresco. It is a holistic socio-economic system in which all goods and services are available without the use of money, credits, barter or any other system of debt or servitude. All resources become the common heritage of all of the inhabitants, not just a select few. The premise upon which this system is based is that the Earth is abundant with plentiful resources; our practice of rationing resources through monetary methods is irrelevant and counterproductive to our survival.*
>
> *Modern society has access to highly advanced technology and can make available food, clothing, housing and medical care; update our educational system; and develop a limitless supply of renewable, non-contaminating energy. By supplying an efficiently designed economy, everyone can enjoy a very high standard of living with all of the amenities of a high technological society.*
>
> *A resource-based economy would utilize existing resources from the land and sea, physical equipment, industrial plants, etc. to enhance the lives of the total population. In an economy based on resources rather than money, we could easily produce all of the necessities of life and provide a high standard of living for all.*
>
> *Consider the following examples: At the beginning of World War II the US had a mere 600 or so first-class fighting aircraft. We rapidly overcame this short supply by turning out more than 90,000 planes a year. The question at the start of World War II*

---

[138] http://www.thevenusproject.com

was: Do we have enough funds to produce the required implements of war? The answer was no, we did not have enough money, nor did we have enough gold; but we did have more than enough resources. It was the available resources that enabled the US to achieve the high production and efficiency required to win the war. Unfortunately this is only considered in times of war.

In a resource-based economy all of the world's resources are held as the common heritage of all of Earth's people, thus eventually outgrowing the need for the artificial boundaries that separate people. This is the unifying imperative.

We must emphasize that this approach to global governance has nothing whatever in common with the present aims of an elite to form a world government with themselves and large corporations at the helm, and the vast majority of the world's population subservient to them. Our vision of globalization empowers each and every person on the planet to be the best they can be, not to live in abject subjugation to a corporate governing body.

Our proposals would not only add to the well-being of people, but they would also provide the necessary information that would enable them to participate in any area of their competence. The measure of success would be based on the fulfillment of one's individual pursuits rather than the acquisition of wealth, property and power.

At present, we have enough material resources to provide a very high standard of living for all of Earth's inhabitants. Only when population exceeds the carrying capacity of the land do many problems such as greed, crime and violence emerge. By overcoming scarcity, most of the crimes and even the prisons of today's society would no longer be necessary.

A resource-based economy would make it possible to use technology to overcome scarce resources by applying renewable sources of energy, computerizing and automating manufacturing and inventory, designing safe energy-efficient cities and advanced transportation systems, providing universal health care and more relevant education, and most of all by generating a new incentive system based on human and environmental concern.

Many people believe that there is too much technology in the world today, and that technology is the major cause of our environmental pollution. This is not the case. It is the abuse and misuse of technology that should be our major concern. In a more humane civilization, instead of machines displacing people they would shorten the workday, increase the availability of goods and services, and lengthen vacation time. If we utilize new technology to raise the standard of living for all people, then the infusion of machine technology would no longer be a threat.

A resource-based world economy would also involve all-out efforts to develop new, clean, and renewable sources of energy: geothermal; controlled fusion; solar; photovoltaic; wind, wave, and tidal power; and even fuel from the oceans. We would eventually be able to have energy in unlimited quantity that could propel civilization for thousands of years. A resource-based economy must also be committed to the redesign of our cities, transportation systems, and industrial plants, allowing them to be energy efficient, clean, and conveniently serve the needs of all people.

What else would a resource-based economy mean? Technology intelligently and efficiently applied, conserves energy, reduces waste, and provides more leisure time. With automated inventory on a global scale, we can maintain a balance between production and distribution. Only nutritious and healthy food would be available and planned obsolescence would be unnecessary and non-existent in a resource-based economy.

As we outgrow the need for professions based on the monetary system, for instance lawyers, bankers, insurance agents, marketing and advertising personnel, salespersons, and stockbrokers, a considerable amount of waste will be eliminated. Considerable amounts of energy would also be saved by eliminating the duplication of competitive products such as tools, eating utensils, pots, pans, and vacuum cleaners. Choice is good. But instead of hundreds of different manufacturing plants and all the paperwork and personnel required to turn out similar products, only a few of the highest quality would be needed to serve the entire population. Our only shortage is the lack of creative thought and intelligence in ourselves and our elected leaders to solve these problems. The most valuable, untapped resource today is human ingenuity.

With the elimination of debt, the fear of losing one's job will no longer be a threat. This assurance, combined with education on how to relate to one another in a much more meaningful way, could considerably reduce both mental and physical stress and leave us free to explore and develop our abilities.

If the thought of eliminating money troubles you, consider this: If a group of people with gold, diamonds and money were stranded on an island that had no resources such as food, clean air and water, their wealth would be irrelevant to their survival. It is only when resources are scarce that money can be used to control their distribution. One could not, for example, sell the air we breathe or water abundantly flowing down from a mountain stream. Although air and water are valuable, in abundance they cannot be sold.

Money is only important in a society when certain resources for survival must be rationed and the people accept money as an exchange medium for the scarce resources. Money is a social convention, an agreement if you will. It is neither a natural resource nor does it represent one. It is not necessary for survival unless we have been conditioned to accept it as such."

Chapter 29. Being Less Dependent on the System

A resource-based economy is ideal, but right now we still live in a monetary-based economy, and if we were to allow the current leaders of society (politicians, bankers, corporations, etc.) to take the lead in this shift to a resource-based economy, it would likely result in a powerful world government that monopolized the resources rather than adequately distributed them amongst the people.

While we should still push toward the idea of a resource-based economy, we need to create change within the current system. People today are too dependent on our modern system for survival. If the electrical grids were to fail, and the system was to crash, people would not know how to act, and many people would not be able to survive.

Regardless of your view of the system, you are a part of it and most likely you depend on it. We need to realize that we are capable of survival without the help of banks, corporations, and governments. Obviously, it would be hard to completely stop contributing to the system, but there are many ways that you can avoid using it to survive. In fact, it is much easier than you think. Following are some ways that can help you begin to assert your independence from the system.

Grow your own food. Growing your own food is like printing your own money. When you grow your own food, you supply your family with meals and help them survive, without the help of a food business. This is how we begin to shift toward a more resource-based economy, by providing our own resources in the safety of our own backyards. Make sure the food you grow is organic and do not use any harmful pesticides or fertilizers. By growing your own food, you can also build a great community. People will work together for the common goal of eating a healthy meal.

A self-sustainable system is a system that can maintain itself by independent effort. Being self-sustainable means that you can provide for yourself by living off of the land and using the resources around you, without the help of a business or corporation. It requires ¼ acre of land to provide enough food for a family of four. Many people do not have ¼ acre of land, but that does not mean you cannot grow food to feed your family, and save money. People have gardens in apartment buildings, on top of skyscrapers, in backyards, and many other areas. As long as you have room for plants to grow in soil and sunlight, then growing your own food should be a priority.

It is possible for many people to become self-sustainable, yet we choose to use the system because we are lazy or do not know any better. Carl Jung, a famous psychologist and naturalist, believed in the idea that man should spend four hours a day contributing toward a common goal, and that the rest of the day should be spent maintaining one's crops. This idea could benefit humanity in many ways. Instead of working pointless jobs, supporting big businesses, humans would work toward goals that benefit humanity, while still having time during the day to provide food and live off of the land.

The reason that people were so independent and free during the early years of America was because they were self-sustainable. The majority of people owned large properties, with crops and other resources readily available to them. Since the industrialization of the world, people have been able to live without large properties because the resources they need could be delivered to them. Without a second thought, this became the new way of life for modern society. It allowed the population to grow rapidly. What people fail to realize is that the resources will not always be available. Eventually the system will crash; it is inevitable, because it is an unsustainable equation. There will come a time when there will not be enough resources to match the population growth.

Right now the human population is over seven billion. We are not the only species living on this planet. We need to be responsible in rationing our resources, and be responsible with the growth of our population. There is no need to have multiple kids that you cannot afford to properly raise. That is no life for you or your child.

Many children are raised in poverty. They develop based on their surroundings, learning from their environment. If they live in a negative environment, odds are they will lead negative lives. That will only contribute to the ignorant state that we are already in. We need to raise our children to be open-minded and intelligent. The future is in the hands of the youth; if we set a good example of love, peace, honesty, and justice, they will be raised to do the same.

Shop Locally. Another way you can be less dependent on the system is by shopping locally and buying from small, independent suppliers. By shopping locally and not buying from the dominant supermarkets, you boycott corporations, making them lose money. Corporations depend on us to keep them powerful. If we do not buy from them, we do not give them any power over us. Shop local as often as you can, and spend as little as you can. There are many local farms, farmer's markets and organic stores that can provide healthy food, without contributing to corporations. Research the stores that you support with your money, and see if they are beneficial to the good of humanity or if they are harmful.

Turn Off the TV. You don't have to give up television and movies altogether, but be alert and aware of the messages and the time you are spending watching it, and always ask yourself if this time could be better spent on other pursuits (the answer most of the time will be 'yes'). The media uses television to inflict feelings of fear and doubt, influence propaganda, distract and misinform the public.

Television is a distraction and it lowers the intelligence of those who watch it. Your conscious mind might know you are watching TV, but your subconscious acts like television is a reality, and absorbs the information as if it were happening in real life. Television is also a way that corporations advertise and influence people into buying their products. If we can refrain from buying things from corporations, it will give them less power over our daily lives.

Self-Educate. By educating yourself, you determine for yourself what is right or wrong. You research the facts and you experience truth first-hand. This is much better than accepting what people tell you, or learning from a schoolteacher. Question everything, and only come to conclusions when you have absolute proof. Do not believe anything I say in this book until you do the research yourself. I encourage you to do so, so that you can get a better understanding of these concepts.

Recycle More. By recycling more often, you reduce your amount of consumption and ultimately reduce your amount of waste. Something as simple as separating your garbage, throwing recyclables into the recycle bin and waste products into the garbage, can have a huge impact on the environment. There are many other ways you can recycle in addition to properly disposing of waste. By reusing old household items and other objects, you can make use of what you already have, saving you money, and reducing the amount of waste you produce.

Return to Nature. We have been raised to live in an artificial environment. Nature does not consist of concrete, roads, skyscrapers, buildings, advertisements, simulations, stock markets, and other superficial things. Nature follows natural systems, it supports life, provides food and water, it is wild, inspires freedom, requires strength, and sustains its inhabitants. Nature is real, it is all that exists, and is the reason that we exist. We are nature, and we depend on nature. By building artificial systems, we block ourselves off from nature. That does not mean nature is gone. The weather, the environment, the trees and the sky—that is all nature, and it still affects our daily lives.

"Man is the most insane species. He worships an invisible God and destroys a visible Nature. Unaware that this Nature he's destroying is the God he is worshipping."
– Hubert Reeves

We need to return to nature, and live more natural lifestyles. Live off of the land. Be self-sustainable. Grow your own food. Use your resources. Stop depending on businesses, stores, supermarkets, and corporations. By doing this you can save your money, and use it toward a better purpose. Perhaps trying to influence our society to becoming more resource-based.

Go Homeopathic. Use foods and herbs to heal, like humans have done for centuries. Pharmaceuticals usually do more damage than provide benefits. There are over 100,000 deaths annually due to prescription drugs in the United States alone.[139] Doctors depend on sick people to earn money, so they do not do what is most beneficial to your health. The medical industry is a business, just like the food industry, and the education industry. They all have the primary purpose of making profit.

Appreciate What You Have. By appreciating what you have, you become content, and do not feel like you need more things. Companies always advertise their products to make it seem like you need them, or your life would be much better with them. It is all a scheme to get your money. You don't need expensive clothes or expensive cars. Happiness is not a result of material wealth.

I want you to take a moment to appreciate what you have. Don't just read this, seriously do it. Take a moment to be thankful that you have two eyes that can see. Be thankful for your legs that can walk. Be grateful for the people in your life, the family that you have. Appreciate the food you eat, the shelter you have and the water you drink. Appreciate the clothes you wear, the life you live, and the things you love. Many people do not appreciate what they have until it's gone. Appreciate what you have while you still have it, because in a few years, months or even days, it will all be different.

When you take a moment to appreciate all that you have, more things will come to you in abundance. This is a great benefit of appreciation, but it is not the point. The point is to realize the things that you have and how fortunate you are to have them. Life is such a precious experience; do not waste it being ungrateful or unsatisfied with what you have. Appreciate everything and show gratitude, even to the things and people that you do not necessarily like. They are still a part of your life, and you learn from everything and everyone you come in contact with. Count your blessings and encourage others to do the same. This is how we shift from a

---

[139] http://www.alternet.org/story/147318/100,000_americans_die_each_year_from_prescription_drugs,_while_pharma_companies_get_rich

negative society of greed, dissatisfaction, and consumption to a more loving and respectful humanity.

Chapter 30. Saving Energy and Reducing Pollution

Renewable energy sources are energy sources that are continually replenished. These include energy from water, wind, the sun, geothermal sources, and biomass sources such as energy crops. In contrast, fuels such as coal, oil, and natural gas are non-renewable. Once a deposit of these fuels is depleted it cannot be replenished—a replacement deposit must be found instead.

Renewable sources of energy vary widely in their cost-effectiveness and in their availability across the United States. Although water, wind, and other renewables may appear free, their cost comes in collecting, harnessing, and transporting the energy so that it can do useful work. For example, to utilize energy from water, a dam must be built along with electric generators and transmission lines.

Renewables themselves are non-polluting, while the structures built to harness them can have positive or negative environmental impacts. For example, dams may affect fish migration but may also create wildlife habitat.

Hydropower

Hydropower refers to using water to generate electricity. Water is the most common renewable source of energy in the United States today.

Many hydroelectric power plants use a dam on a river to store water. Water released from behind the dam flows through a turbine, spinning it, which then turns a generator to produce electricity. Electricity generated this way is known as hydroelectricity, and it accounts for about 7% of the electricity used by the nation.[140] Hydroelectric power doesn't necessarily require a large dam—some hydroelectric power plants just use a small canal to channel the river water through a turbine. A small or micro-hydroelectric power system can produce enough electricity for a home, farm, or ranch.

Wind

For hundreds of years, humans have used wind to pump water or grind grain, usually with small windmills. Large, modern wind turbines are used to generate electricity, either for individual use or for contribution to a utility power grid. Wind turbines usually have two or three blades and, because winds above the ground tend to be faster and less turbulent than those near the surface, the turbines are mounted on tall towers to capture the most energy. As the blades turn, the central shaft spins a generator to make electricity.

In recent years, wind has become an increasingly attractive source of renewable energy; wind energy is the world's fastest-growing energy technology.[141] Wind turbines placed at sites with strong, steady winds can economically generate electricity without producing pollutants. The power in wind increases rapidly with its speed, which means that locating windmills in areas of strong winds is critical. The strongest winds in the United States tend to be in Alaska, the western United States, and the Appalachians. Wind power currently supplies about 1% of United States' electricity needs, but capacity is expanding rapidly.

---

[140] http://www.altenergy.org/renewables/renewables.html

[141] http://windenergyfoundation.org/about-wind-energy/

Solar

Solar technologies use the sun's energy to provide heat, light, hot water, electricity, and even cooling, for homes, businesses, and industry. Despite sunlight's significant potential for supplying energy, solar power provides less than 1% of U.S. energy needs. This percentage is expected to increase with the development of new and more efficient solar technologies.[142]

Different types of solar collectors are used to meet different energy needs. Passive solar building designs capture the sun's heat to provide space heating and light. Photovoltaic cells convert sunlight directly to electricity. Concentrating solar power systems focus sunlight with mirrors to create a high-intensity heat source, which then produces steam or mechanical power to run a generator that creates electricity. Flat-plate collectors absorb the sun's heat directly into water or other fluids to provide hot water or space heating. And solar process heating and cooling systems use specialized solar collectors and chemical processes to meet large-scale hot water and heating and cooling needs.

Geothermal

Geothermal power uses the natural sources of heat inside the Earth to produce heat or electricity. Currently, most geothermal power is generated

---

142 http://dailycaller.com/2014/12/11/solar-energy-will-produce-less-than-one-percent-of-us-power-in-2015/

using steam or hot water from underground. Geothermal power generation produces few emissions and the power source is continuously available.[143]

There are three geothermal technologies currently in use in the United States: direct-use systems, use of deep reservoirs to generate electricity, and geothermal heat pumps.

In direct-use geothermal systems, a well is drilled into a geothermal reservoir to provide a steady stream of hot water. The water is brought up through the well, and a mechanical system—piping, a heat exchanger, and controls—delivers the heat directly for its intended use. A disposal system then either injects the cooled water underground or disposes of it in a surface storage pond. Geothermal hot water is used for heating buildings, raising plants in greenhouses, drying crops, heating water for fish farms, or for industrial processes, at hundreds of sites around the country. Geothermal reservoirs appropriate for direct-use systems are widespread throughout the western United States.

Biomass

Biomass power is power obtained from the energy in plants and plant-derived materials, such as food crops, grassy and woody plants, residues from agriculture or forestry, and the organic component of municipal and industrial wastes.[144] Biomass power provides two valuable services: it is the second most important source of renewable energy in the United States, and it is an important part of our waste management infrastructure. In the future, farms cultivating high-yielding energy crops (such as trees and

---

143 http://www.renewableenergyworld.com/geothermal-energy/tech.html
144 http://www.reenergyholdings.com/renewable-energy/what-is-biomass/

grasses) will significantly expand our supply of biomass. These energy crops, coupled with high-efficiency conversion technologies, can supplement our consumption of fossil fuels and help us respond to global climate change concerns.

Wood has been used for energy longer than any other biomass source and today is still the largest biomass energy resource. The largest source of energy from wood is pulping liquor or "black liquor," a waste product from processes of the pulp, paper, and paperboard industry. Biomass energy can also be derived from waste and from alcohol fuels. Waste energy is the second-largest source of biomass energy. The main contributors of waste energy are municipal solid waste, manufacturing waste, and landfill gas.

Biomass can be used for direct heating (such as burning wood in a fireplace or wood stove), for generating electricity, or can be converted directly into liquid fuels to meet transportation energy needs.

Biomass power is close to a carbon-neutral electric power generation option—biomass absorbs carbon dioxide from the atmosphere during its growth and then emits an equal amount of carbon dioxide when it is processed to generate electricity. Thus, biomass fuels "recycle" atmospheric carbon, and may reduce global warming impacts. Biopower facilities produce fewer other pollutants than equivalent fossil fuel power facilities.

There are plenty of other sources that we can use for energy; sources that do not pollute the planet and can be reused continuously. The need for renewable energy sources is evident. Renewable energy is becoming widely used by people all over the world. The reason that renewable energy sources are not already being used as mainstream resources is because the oil companies have a monopoly over the energy industry. But renewable energy is expanding as more people demand cleaner and more efficient sources of energy.

Renewable energy sources reduce the amount of pollution created by humans, which is a necessity in our modern consumerist society. The goal for every individual should be to create as little waste as possible. One way that businesses can help us achieve this is by producing Biodegradable products.

Biodegradable Products

Biodegradable products are products capable of being decomposed by bacteria or other living organisms. They naturally decompose into the Earth, leaving behind little to no pollution. The goal of supplementing biodegradable products into our everyday lives is to recycle our natural resources and keep the Earth clean and free of growing landfills. We can choose to use many different biodegradable products that will reduce pollution and, as companies notice the demand for these products, they will have no choice but to create biodegradable products or risk going out of business. Companies must keep up with popular markets; if we increase the popularity of biodegradable products, companies will have to meet their customers' demands.

There are plenty of materials we can use that will not pollute the environment. Paper, cotton, linen, wool, silk, wood, beeswax, and hemp are all examples of biodegradable products. Aside from creating biodegradable waste products, we also need to rebuild our modern structures with materials that do not harm the environment.

Hempcrete

Hempcrete is a building material that incorporates hemp into its mixture. Hempcrete is very versatile as it can be used for wall insulation, flooring, walls, roofing and more. It's fireproof, waterproof, and rot-proof as long as it's above ground. Hempcrete is made from the shiv or inside stem of the hemp plant and is then mixed with a lime-based binder to create the building material. This mixture creates a negative carbon footprint so it is not harmful to the environment. Hempcrete is much more versatile, easy to work with and pliable than concrete. In fact, earthquakes cannot crack these structures, as they are three times more resistant than regular concrete.[145]

Hempcrete is a much more superior building material due to the fact that it is a very strong, lightweight, and breathable material. When used as exterior walls, it lets water in without rotting or damaging the material. In a practical sense, instead of needing to build homes with space between exterior walls, which are then filled with insulation, you can simply use a Hempcrete wall. As humidity is taken in from the external environment, the Hempcrete holds that humidity until it is ready to be released again when the climate is less humid.

Since the lime is wrapped in cellulose, the lime takes a bit longer for it to fully petrify, but is still incredibly strong. Over time, the lime looks to turn back to a rock, so the material becomes harder and harder until it petrifies completely. This means the wall will last thousands of years—vs. 40-100, like normal building materials today. Another great aspect of Hempcrete

---

[145] http://www.hemp-technologies.com/page15/page16/page16.html

is that if too much is mixed during building; you can return it to the soil as a great fertilizer. Since hemp grows to maturity in just 14 weeks, it is a very powerful, versatile, cheap, and sustainable solution.

Cob Building

Earth is still probably the world's most common building material. Over 50% of the world's population lives in houses made from mud. Cob building uses hands and feet to form lumps of earth mixed with sand and straw, a sensory and aesthetic experience similar to sculpting with clay. The word cob comes from an old English root meaning "a lump or rounded mass." Cob is easy to learn to use and inexpensive to build with. Because there are no forms, ramming cement or rectangular blocks, cob lends itself to organic shapes: curved walls, arches and niches.

Cob is a mixture of clay, sand, straw, and water.[146] Clay is the binder, sand gives the mixture strength, straw provides tensile strength, and water helps activate the clay to hold the mixture together while building. When the material dries, it becomes hard like cement. Cob homes are cool in the summer and warm in winter. Cobs resistance to rain and cold makes it ideally suited to cold climates like the Pacific Northwest, and to desert conditions. Cob has been used for millennia, even in the harsh climates of coastal Britain. This ancient technology doesn't contribute to deforestation, pollution or mining, nor depend on manufactured materials or power tools. Earth is non-toxic and completely recyclable. In this age of environmental degradation, dwindling natural resources, and chemical

[146] https://www.cobcottage.com/whatis

toxins hidden in our homes, it makes sense to return to nature's most abundant, cheap and healthy building material.

By using renewable energy sources to produce environmentally friendly products, we can drastically reduce the amount of waste and pollution created by humans. The methods are out there; all we need to do is start using these methods more to increase their demand. The power is in the hands of the people. We need to utilize these resources to improve the overall health of the planet, and every form of life that depends on it.

Chapter 31. Organic Agriculture

One of the most necessary things that our society needs to accomplish is the shift from conventional agriculture to organic agriculture. Throughout the past 50 years, conventional farming has depleted agricultural land of its nutrients, and polluted the health of humans, and the planet, through the use of chemical fertilizers and pesticides.

The fertilizers and pesticides that are used to produce crops are bad for the soil. Soil requires soil life to be productive. Microscopic soil organisms ingest other organisms or parts of organisms, both alive and dead, and in their guts break their meal down into its component parts. They excrete some of these parts and use others to maintain their own metabolism until they, in turn, are eaten.

Soil microbes are important not just because they recycle and reconfigure nutrients; they also manufacture and leave behind a variety of vitamins, amino acids, sugars, and other substances beneficial to other soil life forms and to plants. Without soil life, the soil does not have the nutrients it needs to produce plant life. Chemical fertilizers create an artificial source of nutrients for plants while killing the soil life that plants naturally depend on. Farmers have depleted their soil to the point that many of them are now completely dependent on fertilizers to produce crops.

We are depleting the Earth of its nutrients by using chemicals. Farmers all over the globe are doing this. It is estimated that 45-60% of all agricultural land is depleted to some extent.[147]

---

[147] http://www.amazon.com/The-Organic-Farming-Manual-Comprehensive/dp/1603424792

Soil is the element that makes life possible; if all of it is depleted, then we are destroying the opportunity of life for future generations, for all of the animals that depend on it, and for ourselves.

Organic agriculture is a production system that is managed to respond to site-specific conditions by integrating cultural, biological, and mechanical practices that foster cycling of resources, promote ecological balance, and conserve biodiversity.[148] Organic farming prohibits the use of man-made pesticides, herbicides, and fertilizers, as well as antibiotics, hormone treatments, genetically modified organisms, sewage sludge, and the feeding of animal by-products to livestock. Organic farming uses methods that maintain and improve the soil and the ecosystem instead of degrading them. To do this, organic farmers look at the farm as an integrated whole, where all parts of the farm are cared for with the health of all other parts kept in mind.

Organic farming creates a living ecosystem on the land, one that benefits the soil, the plant life, and all of the species that depend on the land. By shifting the agriculture industry into an organic industry, we can regenerate the ecosystems of all of the planet's depleted land. Each ecosystem contributes to the health of the ecosystem it is a part of. All life on Earth is interconnected, and by improving the fertility of each individual piece of land, we are contributing to the overall health of the planet. All people responsible for portions of land should follow the practices of organic farming. Even you can improve the health of the ecosystem in your backyard or garden. By using organic methods of crop production, we can

---

[148] http://www.usda.gov/wps/portal/usda/usdahome?contentidonly=true&contentid=organic-agriculture.html

improve the health of the soil, insects, animals, plants, food, people, and planet as a whole.

Chapter 32. Permaculture

In our early history, agriculture provided the means for civilized life. The central focus of civilization was to maintain the crops and ensure that the entire community received adequate nourishment. By becoming city-dwellers, we have drifted away from this core principle of civilization. As the damaging effects of neglecting our food supply are becoming more and more apparent, it is clear that humanity needs to return our central focus to the production and distribution of healthy food.

Permaculture (permanent agriculture) is an agricultural system that focuses on the natural way of practicing agriculture, maintaining the ecological system, and not strictly adhering to the systems followed in modern agriculture.[149] Permaculture has been defined by many as, "a philosophy of working with, rather than against nature; of protracted and thoughtful observation rather than protracted and thoughtless labor; and of looking at plants and animals in all their functions, rather than treating any area as a single project system."

Permaculture is a creative design process that is based on ethics and design principles. It guides us to mimic the patterns and relationships we find in nature and apply them to all aspects of human habitation, from agriculture to ecological building, from appropriate technology to education and even economics.

---

149 http://permacultureprinciples.com/

By adopting the ethics and applying these principles in our daily life, we can make the transition from being dependent consumers to becoming responsible producers. This journey builds skills and resilience at home and in our local communities that will help us prepare for an uncertain future with less available energy.[150]

The techniques and strategies used to apply these principles vary widely depending on the location, climatic conditions and resources that are available. The methods may differ, but the foundations to this holistic approach remain constant. By learning these principles you can acquire valuable thinking tools that help you become more resilient in an era of change.

Permaculture is a way of designing farms and gardens so that they are integrated with their environment. This involves growing foreign and native plants together in a cohesive system, making use of limited space and resources, and many other practices that promote diversity, sustainability, and creativity. The principles followed in permaculture design are listed below.[151]

1. **Observe and Interact** – "Beauty is in the eye of the beholder." By taking the time to engage with nature, we can design solutions that suit our particular situation.
2. **Catch and Store Energy** – "Make hay while the sun shines." By developing systems that collect resources when they are abundant, we can use them in times of need.
3. **Obtain a yield** – "You can't work on an empty stomach." Ensure that you are getting truly useful rewards as part of the work you are doing.

---

[150] http://www.permaculture.org/

[151] https://prezi.com/jyago6a5lj5o/permaculture-principles/

4. **Apply Self-Regulation and Accept Feedback** – "The sins of the father are visited on the children."
   We need to discourage inappropriate activity to ensure that systems can continue to function well. Negative feedback is often slow to emerge.
5. **Use and Value Renewable Resources and Services** – "Let nature take its course."
   Make the best use of Nature's abundance to reduce our consumptive behavior and dependence on non-renewable resources.
6. **Produce No Waste** – "Waste not, want not" or "A stitch in time saves nine."
   By valuing and making use of all the resources that are available to us, nothing goes to waste.
7. **Design from Patterns to Details** – "Can't see the forest for the trees."
   By stepping back, we can observe patterns in nature and society. These can form the backbone of our designs, with the details filled in as we go.
8. **Integrate Rather Than Segregate** – "Many hands make light work."
   By putting the right things in the right place, relationships develop between those things, and they work together to support each other.
9. **Use Small and Slow Solutions** – "Slow and steady wins the race" or "The bigger they are, the harder they fall."
   Small and slow systems are easier to maintain than big ones, making better use of local resources and producing more sustainable outcomes.
10. **Use and Value Diversity** – "Don't put all your eggs in one basket."
    Diversity reduces vulnerability to a variety of threats and takes advantage of the unique nature of the environment in which it resides.
11. **Use Edges and Value the Marginal** – "Don't think you are on the right track just because it's a well-beaten path."
    The interface between things is where the most interesting events take place. These are often the most valuable, diverse and productive elements in the system.
12. **Creatively Use and Respond to Change** – "Vision is not seeing things as they are but as they will be"

> We can have a positive impact on inevitable change by carefully observing and then intervening at the right time.

Permaculture is the most efficient way to produce food for our species, while promoting the health of the soil, all life and the planet as a whole. By using all the natural components of the ecosystem (like composting the waste into useful organic matter and manure), you save up a lot of money, which you would otherwise be spending on conventional farming.

In permaculture, the waste products are recycled back to the Earth in the form of compost. Once you start following this practice, the waste material is later used as a natural fertilizer. There is less waste because all the present resources are optimally utilized.

Permaculture also decreases the amount of pollution created by humans. If you are using the most natural way of agricultural cultivation, then there is no way you can increase the pollution. In fact, the zone in which permaculture is practiced will be pollution free.

Permaculture promotes green living. In permaculture, one uses natural fertilizers, natural pesticides, and freshwater reserves. It teaches us different ways of attaining sufficient and sustainable agriculture in a way beneficial for the environment. Those who follow this culture, produce agricultural goods using a harmonious integration of human dwellings, microclimate, plants, animals, soil, and water in a productive and stable way.

One of the best ways that we can protect the environment is by building healthy environments in our own backyards. Permaculture, homesteading, and other natural farming methods focus on building the health of the land, and all life that depends on that land.

Conventional agriculture destroys soil, is not regulated, is controlled by corporations, is not sustainable, degrades natural balance, is 100% less efficient, and produces food with fewer nutrients. Permaculture however, works with nature, rather than against it, produces food with a high nutritional value, is all natural and low maintenance, creates useful products (food, fuel, fiber, forage, herbs, spices, poles, medicines, honey, dye plants, basketry material, seeds, income), produces biodiversity, is resilient and strong, maximizes life, recycles energy, and produces no waste.

The system and the concepts followed in permaculture sound very promising in maintaining the ecological system well and also in bringing self-reliance to farmers, by means of implementing sustainable and productive farms and gardens. It is essentially about going back to the traditional method of farming, incorporating the features of organic farming, agro-forestry, sustainable development, and applied ecology. With all of the disasters created by humans, there really seems no other way of saving the Earth.

"Permaculture is revolution disguised as gardening."
– Mike Feingold

Chapter 33. Hemp

Many people have a negative view of marijuana, and even consider it to be a "drug." Most people's opinions of marijuana are based on propaganda and misinformation. Marijuana is a plant, and this amazing plant can be used for so many things. The flower of the plant (Cannabis) can be used to benefit health, and the plant itself (Hemp) has thousands of industrial purposes. Before going into the benefits of marijuana, I would like to discuss the history and the lies that have been associated with it.[152]

American production of hemp was encouraged by the government in the 17th century for the production of rope, sails, and clothing.[153] The Virginia Company, by decree of King James I in 1619, ordered every colonist to grow 100 plants specifically for export. Therefore, England's only colony in America began to grow hemp in order to meet this obligation and, soon, to serve a growing demand in other colonies. George Washington grew hemp at Mount Vernon as one of his three primary crops.

Domestic production flourished until after the Civil War, when imports and other domestic materials replaced hemp for many purposes. In the late nineteenth century, marijuana became a popular ingredient in many medicinal products and was sold openly in public pharmacies. During the 19th century, hashish use became a fad in France and also, to some extent, in the U.S.

---

[152] http://www.hemp.com/history-of-hemp/

[153] http://hempethics.weebly.com/what-is-industrial-hemp.html

After the Mexican Revolution of 1910, Mexican immigrants flooded into the U.S., introducing to American culture the recreational use of marijuana. The plant then became associated with the immigrants, and the fear and prejudice about the Spanish-speaking newcomers became associated with marijuana. Anti-drug campaigners warned against the encroaching "Marijuana Menace," and terrible crimes were attributed to marijuana and the Mexicans who used it.

During the Great Depression, massive unemployment increased public resentment and fear of Mexican immigrants, escalating public and governmental concern about the problem of marijuana. This instigated a flurry of research that linked the use of marijuana with violence, crime, and other socially deviant behaviors, primarily committed by "racially inferior" or underclass communities. By 1931, 29 states had outlawed marijuana.

Concern about the rising use of marijuana and research linking its use with crime and other social problems created pressure on the federal government to take action. Rather than promoting federal legislation, the Federal Bureau of Narcotics strongly encouraged state governments to accept responsibility for control of the problem by adopting the Uniform State Narcotic Act.

After a scandalous national propaganda campaign against the "evil weed," Congress passed the Marijuana Tax Act. The law effectively criminalized marijuana, restricting possession of the drug to individuals who paid an excise tax for certain authorized medical and industrial uses.

In 1944, the New York Academy of Medicine issued an extensively researched report declaring that, contrary to earlier research and popular belief, use of marijuana did not induce violence, insanity or sex crimes, or lead to addiction or other drug use.

During World War II, imports of hemp and other materials crucial for producing marine cordage, parachutes, and other military necessities became scarce. In response, the U.S. Department of Agriculture launched its "Hemp for Victory" program, encouraging farmers to plant hemp by giving out seeds and granting draft deferments to those who would stay home and grow hemp. By 1943, American farmers registered in the program harvested 375,000 acres of hemp.

In the 1960s, a changing political and cultural climate was reflected in more lenient attitudes towards marijuana. Use of the drug became widespread in the white upper-middle class. Reports commissioned by Presidents Kennedy and Johnson found that marijuana use did not induce violence nor lead to use of heavier drugs. Policy towards marijuana began to involve considerations of treatment as well as criminal penalties.

In 1970, congress repealed most of the mandatory penalties for drug-related offenses. It was widely acknowledged that the mandatory minimum sentences of the 1950s had done nothing to eliminate the drug culture that embraced marijuana use throughout the 60s, and that the minimum sentences imposed were often excessively harsh.

In 1976, a nationwide movement emerged of conservative parents' groups lobbying for stricter regulation of marijuana and the prevention of drug use by teenagers. Some of these groups became quite powerful and, with the support of the Drug Enforcement Agency (DEA) and the National Institute on Drug Abuse (NIDA), were instrumental in affecting public attitudes that led to the 1980s' War on Drugs.

In 1986, President Reagan signed the Anti-Drug Abuse Act, instituting mandatory sentences for drug-related crimes. In conjunction with the Comprehensive Crime Control Act of 1984, the new law raised federal penalties for marijuana possession and dealing, basing the penalties on the amount of the drugs involved. Possession of 100 marijuana plants received the same penalty as possession of 100 grams of heroin. A later amendment to the Anti-Drug Abuse Act established a "three strikes and you're out" policy, requiring life sentences for repeat drug offenders, and providing the death penalty for "drug kingpins."

In 1996, California voters passed Proposition 215, allowing for the sale and medical use of marijuana for patients with AIDS, cancer, and other serious and painful diseases. This law stands in opposition to Federal laws prohibiting possession of marijuana. California was the first state to introduce medical marijuana, and since then the industry has flourished. Today, laws have even passed seeing marijuana as a legal drug for recreational use. Marijuana legalization won on the ballot in Colorado and Washington in the 2012 election, and in Alaska, Oregon and Washington, D.C., in the 2014 election.

The history of marijuana is very controversial. It is widely acknowledged that the plant has numerous benefits both for health and industrial purposes, yet the propaganda of the 20th century managed to shape public opinion into believing the plant is a harmful drug. Countless famous and successful people have smoked marijuana, including Bill Gates, Carl Sagan, Morgan Freeman, Oprah Winfrey, Barack Obama, Bill Clinton and many others.

"The illegality of cannabis is outrageous, an impediment to full utilization of a drug which helps produce the serenity and insight, sensitivity and fellowship so desperately needed in this increasingly mad and dangerous world."

– Carl Sagan

The medicinal use of marijuana comes from the flower of the plant, known as cannabis. Cannabis has numerous health benefits and has been known to cure many diseases. It is used to treat glaucoma, improve lung health, control epileptic seizures, decrease symptoms in Dravet's Syndrome, decrease anxiety, slow the progression of Alzheimer's disease, eliminate Crohn's disease, soothe tremors for people with Parkinson's disease, help veterans with PTSD, prevent concussions and brain trauma, decrease pain of multiple sclerosis, reduce muscle spasms, lessen side effects of hepatitis C, treat inflammatory bowel disease, relieve arthritis, improve metabolism, improve symptoms of lupus, and stop cancer from spreading.[154] [155]

There have been frequent cases in which cancer patients document the use of concentrated amounts of THC (the active chemical in cannabis) in curing their disease. Many doctors and health professionals know this, but cancer is a multi-billion dollar industry, and as evil as it seems, it is not profitable to cure cancer. This is another example of the greed for profit that is destructive to humanity.

Patent US6630507 is a U.S. patent that proves the benefits of medicinal cannabis are acknowledged by the Federal government. This next paragraph is cited directly from the patent:

> *"Cannabinoids have been found to have antioxidant properties, unrelated to NMDA receptor antagonism. This newfound property makes cannabinoids useful in the treatment and prophylaxis of wide variety of oxidation associated diseases, such as ischemic, age-related, inflammatory and autoimmune diseases. The cannabinoids are*

---

[154] http://www.thehempconsultants.com/Hemp_as_a_Medicine.php

[155] http://druglibrary.org/schaffer/hemp/medhemp1.htm

> *found to have particular application as neuroprotectants, for example in limiting neurological damage following ischemic insults, such as stroke and trauma, or in the treatment of neurodegenerative diseases, such as Alzheimer's disease, Parkinson's disease and HIV dementia. Nonpsychoactive cannabinoids, such as cannabidiol, are particularly advantageous to use because they avoid toxicity that is encountered with psychoactive cannabinoids at high doses useful in the method of the present invention. A particular disclosed class of cannabinoids useful as neuroprotective antioxidants is formula (I) wherein the R group is independently selected from the group consisting of H, CH_3, and $COCH_3$."*[156]

Clearly the Federal Government recognizes the benefits of cannabis, yet it is still illegal on a Federal level. Contrary to popular belief, cannabis has many health benefits, and has been proven to cure numerous diseases.[157]

The recreational use of cannabis is primarily a method of relaxation, but it also brings many people together from different cultural backgrounds. Contrary to stereotypes, marijuana usage has also been shown to have some positive mental effects, particularly in terms of increasing creativity. Even though people's short-term memories tend to function worse when under the influence, people get better at tests requiring them to come up with new ideas.

Now, I am not promoting the recreational use of marijuana, but I do believe that most of the claims towards the recreational use of this plant are excessive and lack reasonable thinking. There has not been a single death linked directly to the use of marijuana and its effect on the body.

---

[156] http://www.google.com/patents/US20130059018

[157] http://www.collective-evolution.com/2013/08/23/20-medical-studies-that-prove-cannabis-can-cure-cancer/

Compared to alcohol and tobacco, marijuana seems like the healthier alternative for a recreational substance, although that does not mean marijuana does not have any negative effects. I believe the biggest harm marijuana can cause is a severe lack of ambition amongst frequent users. We need our energy and ambition for the will to complete everyday tasks. Marijuana is often used as a scapegoat to avoid these tasks, which can have serious repercussions if not used responsibly.

Aside from the many health benefits and recreational uses provided by marijuana, the plant is most useful for its industrial purposes. The industrial use of marijuana comes from the fiber of the plant, which is extracted from the stem. With the help of the hemp plant we, as a society could create a cleaner energy source that can replace nuclear power, remove radioactive waste from the soil, and eliminate smog from our skies in more industrialized areas.

The hemp plant could assist in eliminating non-biodegradable plastics and cars by reintroducing Henry Ford's 100 year old dream of building cars made from hemp with a plastic hemp car body that can withstand a blow 10 times as great as steel without denting, weighs 1 thousand pounds less than steel, therefore improving gas mileage, can run on a vegetable oil based all-natural hemp fuel, and has a completely biodegradable body. Nationwide hemp production could eliminate deforestation by converting current paper to hemp paper which can be recycled up to eight times, whereas our current wood pulp is only recyclable up to three times, and we could thrive from eating hemp seeds and feeding it to our animals.

Industrial hemp can make our future roads, highways and freeways from hemp-based concrete, which lasts for centuries. Society can benefit from the hemp plant's attributes (such as oxygen production), hemp's dense root structure, and hemp's nutrient and nitrogen production back into the soil. We could make an estimated 50,000 products ranging from building composites, cellophane, and dynamite to shampoo, textiles, twine and yarn. If the U.S. began to grow industrial hemp, it could stop wars, save the environment, boost our economy, improve general health and well being, virtually end our reliance on any foreign entity, and save humankind from itself.

Studies have shown that hemp's biomass can be converted into energy and could replace nuclear power and our current fossil fuels. Just by farming 6% of the U.S.'s acreage, this could be achieved. Hemp grown in biomass could fuel a trillion-dollar-per-year industry, while at the same time create more jobs, clean our air, and distribute wealth to our communities and away from centralized power monopolies. Hemp's biomass can be converted into gasoline, methanol, and methane at a fraction of the current cost of oil, coal, or nuclear energy.

An article from Montana State University states, "When burned in a diesel engine, bio-diesel replaces the exhaust odor of petroleum diesel with a smell something akin to french-fries. Bio-diesel is 11 percent oxygen by weight and contains no sulfur, so instead of creating sulfur-based smog and acid rain as by-products, it produces 11 percent oxygen instead. Bio-diesel can be made from domestically produced, renewable oilseed crops such as hemp." The hemp grown through government farming and regulation is called "industrialized hemp" and contains no more than 0.03 percent THC content, which is not a high enough percentage for medicinal or recreational use. Canada, China, and England are examples of countries that have never prohibited, but instead have responsibly grown, produced, and thrived off of industrialized hemp.

By using marijuana for its industrial uses as well as its medical uses, we can dramatically improve the state of our society. Marijuana is illegal because it threatens too many other industries. If we were to utilize this plant as a dominant resource, it would threaten many large corporations in the industries of fuel, medicine, food, steel, construction, transportation, agriculture, and numerous others. Marijuana would benefit humanity, but not benefit the corporations that are limiting humanity's potential. It is an obvious decision that we need to make as a society. Decriminalizing marijuana and using it for its exceptional benefits, will help us out of the hole that we have dug ourselves into.

Chapter 34. Unifying Mind and Body

"The training of the mind, educating it and disciplining it in unison with the body, will give us the means by which we may participate as beings – human beings."

– The Dalai Seng Shi

How can we expect to heal the world if we do not first heal ourselves? Society is a reflection of our actions and our behavior, which would explain why our violent and destructive nature correlates with a violent and destructive society.

I cannot stress enough the need for nutrition, exercise, reading, self-education, and discipline in our daily lives. Living in a materialistic society that values consumerism, we have become extremely unsatisfied with who we are. We always seem to want more no matter what we have. We hardly ever appreciate the abundance of things around us that sustain our existence.

The reason that we are so troubled is because of our extreme lack of health, both physically and mentally. Our minds are constantly polluted with irrelevant distractions (media, social networking, television, advertisements, video games, etc.) and as a result we ignore the most fundamental needs of our bodies.

Focusing on nutrition is the first step that we need to take as a society. Understanding where our food comes from, how it is grown, what is in it, and how it effects our health, are essential to maintaining the well-being of our bodies and our culture. Most of us do not have the slightest clue of where our food comes from or how to produce our own food. To really develop a sustainable lifestyle, we must grow our own food. No matter how much food you are able to grow, the knowledge and experience of growing food are fundamental to our survival as a species.

If we want a sustainable society, we all need to lead sustainable lives. It is no secret that our society suffers from an excessive amount of poverty. Many people do not have the space or the resources to produce their own food, which is why, as a community, we should focus on building community gardens. Community gardens will not only bring us closer to each other, but they will bring us closer to Nature and allow us to survive off of the land using the resources around us.

The next best thing that we can do aside from growing our own food is to buy food from local farms and businesses. When you shop locally you boycott large corporations, taking power away from them and restoring it to the people. What we buy determines what is popular for the market. If everybody were to only buy organic food, any other type of food would become a marketing liability, and businesses would be forced to switch to organic food or suffer losing business. By being responsible with our money, we determine the markets, and we determine what is sold in stores. It is up to us to know what is beneficial to our health and what is not.

To do this, we must all have a basic understanding of nutrition. Our bodies require six essential nutrients: carbohydrates, fats, vitamins, protein, minerals, and water. It is important that we get these nutrients from natural and organic sources. Growing our own food is the best way to ensure it is organic, but paying attention to labels and ingredients will also help.

Food is the best medicine. If your body is properly nourished, your immune system can function at its optimal level of performance, preventing you from getting ill. The medical industry does not want people to be healthy because they will have less business, which means they will make less money. Food is preventative medicine, and preventative medicine does not bring doctors business, therefore they focus on prescribing "cures" instead of stopping an illness at the source. The "cures" that doctors prescribe are usually pharmaceutical drugs, which may aid in the recovery of certain ailments but have numerous side effects that are harmful to the rest of your body.

The food we eat determines our overall health and the amount of energy that we have. We cannot get energy from the sun so we get it through plants, which get their energy through photosynthesis. The amount of energy that we have determines how well we are able to participate as human beings. More energy = a better life. When we have the energy that our bodies require to function correctly, we realize just how powerful we are, and that is what the banks and corporations are afraid of. That is why most of our food is full of chemicals, and lacks the nutrients our bodies require. That is also why nutritional science is not a subject commonly taught in public schools.

As human beings we need to stay active. Food gives us the energy we need, but it is up to us to decide what we do with this energy. We all have the same 24-hours each day to do what needs to be done. Spending a majority of your day on the couch or in front of a screen is lazy, unhealthy and counterproductive to our survival. We need to invest our time wisely, promoting our health and the health of our planet. Being accustomed to a lazy lifestyle makes it challenging to work on bettering our health. It requires much discipline, both mentally and physically to reach a level of optimal health, but once at that level we can properly function as human beings and contribute to our society in a much more beneficial way.

Discipline requires personal effort; it cannot be forced upon you. As my Qigong instructor tells me, "I can take you to the edge, but you must make the leap." You have to decide whether you want to master your mind, or allow it to master you.

Taming your mind starts with taming your emotions, knowing how to control your temper and how to properly react to situations. It is easy to speak of peace, but can you remain peaceful when someone is screaming in your face? Practicing how to maintain your inner peace is an essential part of life. Breathing calmly and deeply can help you to maintain peace of mind, even in stressful situations. This is another benefit of meditation, and the more you practice, the easier it is to put to use when necessary. Just remember that you decide how you want to feel. Even if everyone around you is fearful or stressed, this does not mean that you need to tune to their emotional frequency.

"An entire sea of water can't sink a ship unless it gets inside the ship. Similarly, the negativity of the world can't put you down unless you allow it to get inside you."
— Goi Nasu

Our happiness depends on how we think. Many of us have unconsciously been taught how to think. Schools, institutions, media, governments, and other authorities have trained us to determine what method of thinking is acceptable and what is unacceptable. To break free from this mental prison, we must unlearn what we have previously learned.

Disciplining the mind and body to function as one organism, where both are aware of their environment and know how to properly react to it, gives us the means by which we can accurately participate as human beings. I have developed a simple formula to cultivate a balanced lifestyle (and I understand there are many factors involved that make things more complex, nonetheless this simple formula provides a great framework for health and wellness) and that formula is: Healthy soil = healthy food = healthy body = healthy mind = healthy life. It is as simple as that. The health of our soil determines the quality of our food, the quality of our food determines the amount of energy and nutrients our bodies get, the amount of energy and nutrients we get determines our mood and its influence on our thoughts, which in turn create a balanced and healthy lifestyle.

We need to be less dependent on corporations and learn to sustain ourselves if we want to restore the health of our society. By growing our own food, educating ourselves, and using our energy wisely, we can be who we were truly meant to be. Before there can be any global revolution, there must first be a revolution of the mind and the way that we think.

"The most important kind of freedom is to be what you really are. You trade in your reality for a role. You trade in your sense for an act. You give up your ability to feel, and in exchange, put on a mask. There can't be any large-scale revolution until there's a personal revolution, on an individual level. It's got to happen inside first."

— Jim Morrison

Chapter 35. Enlightenment

With the use of the Internet, many more people are getting access to information that has otherwise been hard to obtain. As a result of this, our society is growing towards one that is more educated, with citizens who are more capable of formulating individual opinions. We are also much more connected to each other than ever before. As we obtain new information and connect with more people from different backgrounds, many great realizations occur that alter our perspectives, causing us to see the reality of our existence in a different light. This state of realizing our true nature is often referred to as enlightenment.

Enlightenment is often viewed as a New Age concept, but it is a well-known phenomenon that has been discussed since ancient history, primarily by Eastern civilizations. Enlightenment is about eliminating the ego, your self-constructed image, your false identity; and realizing your true nature, which is our oneness with the universe. It is about expanding your consciousness and level of understanding to embrace the reality that we are not separate from the Universe; we are the Universe experiencing itself. Every atom in your body came from a star that exploded, and these stars all originated from the same source of energy billions of years ago. The Universe is one unified energy; just look at the prefix "Uni" meaning one, and the suffix "verse" meaning the whole range or totality.

There is no boundary separating one subatomic particle from the next; similarly there is no boundary separating you from everything else. The Universe has expanded, but it originates from the same source. We were made from the same energy that created the stars. You are not your name, your resume, your accomplishments, or your ethnic background; you are a part of the whole Universe, just as a wave is a part of the ocean. You breathe without effort, your cells function independently without your control, your mind functions naturally, you are more than just an identity; you are the Universe. When you understand this intuitively and not just intellectually, you will inevitably feel an overwhelming sense of oneness, a realization that you are not a separate entity, that you are an integral piece of your environment. This realization is the mental state that is properly associated with the term enlightenment.

"If you have a golf-ball-sized consciousness, when you read a book, you'll have a golf-ball-sized understanding; when you look out a window, a golf-ball-sized awareness, when you wake up in the morning, a golf-ball-sized wakefulness; and as you go about your day, a golf-ball-sized inner happiness. But if you can expand that consciousness, make it grow, then when you read about that book, you'll have more understanding; when you look out, more awareness; when you wake up, more wakefulness; as you go about your day, more inner happiness. It's consciousness, and there is an ocean of pure vibrant consciousness inside each one of us; and it is at the source and base of mind, right at the source of thought, and it's also at the source of all matter. Maharishi Mahesh Yogi teaches a technique called transcendental meditation, it's a simple, easy, effortless technique, yet supremely profound, that allows any human being to dive within experiencing subtler levels of mind and intellect, and transcend and experience this ocean of pure consciousness. This pure consciousness is called by modern physics the Unified Field, it's at the base of all mind and all matter and modern science now says all of matter, everything that is a thing, emerges from this field – and this field has qualities like bliss, intelligence, creativity, universal love, energy, peace; and it's not the intellectual

understanding of this field but the experience of it that does everything. You dive within, transcending and experiencing this pure field of consciousness – and you enliven it, you unfold it, it grows; - and this final outcome of this growth of consciousness is called enlightenment, and enlightenment is the full potential of all human beings."

– David Lynch on Consciousness, Creativity, and the Brain

The English definition for enlighten is: to give intellectual or spiritual light to. This is only an attempt to put the experience into words. Words cannot explain this state because it requires individual effort to achieve enlightenment; it is something you must experience for yourself. If you want to know the taste of an orange, you have to taste it; no amount of description can exactly convey its taste to you. Similarly, you cannot properly explain enlightenment to someone who has not experienced it. Enlightenment also has many different ways it can be interpreted. Each time you have an experience that broadens your perspective you are essentially being enlightened, though the term is usually associated with the realization of oneness.

An excerpt from "The Shaolin Grandmaster's Text" does an accurate job of explaining enlightenment:

"True spiritual practice leads to a state often known as the "little death," representing a point in time when the person emerges on the other side of a portal of understanding. The event is nothing less than an enlightenment experience, and once through that portal nothing in the world will ever seem quite the same as it was before. This new way of seeing is a path from which there is no going back. Once you have heard a symphony orchestra in person, you might forget the tune, but never the complexity, clarity and magic of the sound. This

is the way of enlightenment, of the expansion of consciousness. You may not see the world the same way ten years later than you did the first day, the fact is that you can't ever see the world as you once did. Buddhists think of this experience as moving past the veil of illusion, because in the pre-enlightenment stages we see only dim images of reality, as if we are viewing the world through a thin curtain.

Once the spiritual path is seen and followed to its intended conclusion, the person has become transformed. The practitioner is still human, but in the moment of enlightenment recognizes that he or she is also everything else, too. We are made of atoms that formed in the core of an exploding sun, the same elements that make up the closest parasite and the farthest quasar. Enlightenment, which comes when we move from knowing about this reality to understanding it, transforms us. We no longer care about such transitory and, ultimately unimportant things (in themselves) such as money, status, politics, or time. This is not divine or supernatural position, but a simple recognition that we are neither terribly special nor completely worthless, either. We simply are, and that state of being is without time or place. Only our temporary form and way of perceiving our nature differ from existence to existence."

– Order of Shaolin Ch'an

Enlightenment is not about building a false sense of spirituality or blindly following religious doctrine, it is about carefully cultivating practices that relieve one of the ego and transcend the illusory perceptions of the world. When we get rid of our ego, we stop doing things to impress others, we stop trying to cling to the idea of ourselves and we realize that we are a part of the natural world. This realization will give us the perspective that is greatly needed to improve the state of our society.

Nature is interconnected; when we do damage to one fraction of the web of life, we do damage to the entire web. Everything that we do affects everything else, including ourselves. We cannot ignore the constant pollution and assume it won't interfere with our lives down the road. We need to understand the interconnectedness of Nature and act accordingly if we wish to heal our current situation here on Earth. We need to start treating things in relation to every other thing, especially when it involves life, health, and the use of natural resources.

Another great excerpt from "The Shaolin Grandmaster's Text" provides a precise message of our current situation:

"As with the generations that came before us, we too will face many challenges. Some of these challenges are truly unique in human history, such as global warming and other difficulties enabled by technological advance. Other obstacles to a peaceful and wholesome planet are as ancient as humanity. Wars and diseases readily come to mind. Historical events of old seem to recur in cycles, even if they fail to do so with astronomical precision. The latter half of the twentieth century has been a period of seemingly unbounded prosperity. As a result, many people today harbor a sense of limitless growth for humanity.

Our unbounded growth, however, leads to excessive consumption of natural resources. There is irony here: the same science we use to increase the complexity of our tools and our mastery over the physical universe also informs us that a belief in unbound growth is disconnected from reality. Science tells us that balance will one day come. We can ignore the message, bury our heads in the sand, and eventually collide head on with a harsh and unpleasant future. We can also listen, learn, and exercise our abilities to ensure that our planet is a vibrant and healthy one for ourselves and future generations of plants and animals. Just as we create new problems for ourselves by only listening to scientific deliverances we wish to hear, inattention to our past mistakes and our "it's not my problem" attitude towards exercising compassion sabotages attempts to develop lasting peace. The Buddha's teaching on mindfulness can be of service here. In Shaolin, we are mindful so that we may make appropriate decisions on behalf of ourselves and our communities, yet we also recognize that things get better and worse in a never-ending cycle.

Shaolin is, as we have discussed, a pragmatic school in which hope and serendipity are not acceptable currencies upon which to base decisions. Neither is it a font of unfounded optimism that seeks to make people feel good regardless of circumstances. In its insistence on examining reality and taking measure of multiple variables, Shaolin forces its adherents to look long and hard at the world and to accept the basic reality that all we can change in this lifetime is ourselves. Mahatma Gandhi perhaps said it most eloquently: "We must become the change that we want to see in the world." From this vantage, we may only act as lighthouse-like beacons to others who would walk the path with us. Enough committed souls could effectively modify the future to make it more palatable. The challenge is enormous, for even if changes are made now, today, the number of people and problems we must steer through to ensure adequate food, health care, education, hygiene, and basic human comforts are staggering."

– Order of Shaolin Ch'an

We could learn a lot from the philosophy of Shaolin. Their belief that the ego must be transcended in order to focus on reality is an essential lesson that applies to all of humanity. We could also benefit greatly from their philosophy of independence, individualism and self-reliance. Instead of depending on governments and corporations, we should depend on our environment, our compassionate human interaction, and ourselves. To do this, we must practice what we preach. It is easy to speak of ways to heal the world, but to actually act accordingly is much more difficult. It will take great courage for us to change our way of life and shift toward a more sustainable society, but it must be done if we are to cultivate a peaceful and loving civilization.

"However many holy words you read,
however many you speak, what good will they do
if you do not act on upon them?"
– Gautama Buddha

Chapter 36. The Path of Health

As a society and as individuals, our ultimate goal should be that of optimal health. By living a healthy lifestyle and doing what is best for our bodies, we will ultimately do what is best for our planet as well.

To keep up with the demand for food, and to make sure that the global population receives adequate nourishment, as a species, we must stop the practice of producing and consuming animal products, and replace our diet with an organic plant-based diet. By doing so, we will stop much environmental pollution and the torture of animal life while sparking a global epidemic of health.

We cannot expect our governments and corporations to support this necessary change. If the global population stopped consuming animal products, it would have a severe impact on the meat industry as well as the medical industry that depends on your consumption of meat and poor state of health for profit. These are multi-billion dollar industries; the corporations will never admit that our diet has the largest impact over our health and environment.

In 1812, there were 1 billion people on the planet. In 1912, there were 1.5 billion. By 2012, the global population more than tripled, reaching a massive 7 billion people. A lot of resources are required to sustain 7 billion people. Earth has a finite amount of resources, and the management and distribution of the planet's resources should be done wisely.

Currently, our method of resource distribution is completely unsustainable. There are more than 70 billion farm animals being raised today. The human population drinks 5.2 billion gallons of water every day and consumes 21 billion pounds of food, while the world's 1.5 billion cattle alone drink 45 billion gallons of water and eat 135 billion pounds of food per day. We are growing enough food to feed nearly 15 billion people, but still roughly a billion people are starving every day. Worldwide, 50% of the grain and legumes being grown are fed to livestock.

You can produce 15 times more protein from plant-based sources than you can from meat on any given area of land. Why do we not grow food for humans on the same land where we are growing food for animals?

A plant-based diet is the most sustainable diet for wisely consuming the planet's resources. To feed a person for a whole year on a completely vegan diet requires just 1/6 acre of land. To feed an average American citizen's high-consumption diet of meat, eggs, and dairy requires 18 times the amount of land. In one year, you can grow 37,000 pounds of vegetables on 1.5 acres, but can only produce 375 pounds of meat. A vegan diet also produces half as much CO2 as an American omnivore's, uses 1/11 the amount of fossil fuels, 1/13 the amount of water, and 1/18 the amount of land.

Waste from animal agriculture is the largest producer of methane. Methane is 25-100 times more destructive than CO2, and has a global warming power 866 times that of CO2. Livestock is also responsible for 65% of all emissions of nitrous oxide, a greenhouse gas 296 times more destructive than carbon dioxide that stays in the atmosphere for 150 years. The emissions for agriculture are expected to increase 80% by 2050.[158]

Animal agriculture use ranges from 34-76 trillion gallons of water annually. Agriculture is responsible for 80-90% of U.S. water consumption; 2,500 gallons of water are needed to produce just 1 pound of beef.

---

[158] http://www.cowspiracy.com/facts

Livestock covers 45% of the Earth's total land. Over 136 million rainforest acres have already been cleared for animal agriculture. Animal agriculture is the leading cause of species extinction, ocean dead zones, water pollution and habitat destruction. If we truly wanted to save the planet and reverse the damages we have done, we would take responsibility for our actions and switch to a plant-based diet. Every time that we buy meat we are supporting the animal agriculture industry and contributing to the destruction of our planet's resources.

If we didn't kill all of these animals and eat them, then we wouldn't have to breed all of these cows, pigs, chickens, and other livestock. If we didn't breed these animals, then we wouldn't have to feed these animals. If we didn't have to feed them, we wouldn't have to devote all of the land to growing grains and legumes to feed to them. So then the forest could come back, wildlife could return, ocean life would return, the rivers would be clean again, the air would be clean again, and our health would return. This is achievable by switching to a plant-based diet and encouraging other people to do the same. Educate yourself and others. Show them that there are delicious and nutritious alternatives to eating meat, and that by eating meat they are contributing to the pollution of the planet. There are plenty of plant foods that will provide you with more than enough nutrients to be healthy.

Many people hold a strong emotional attachment to their food. They were raised to eat the way they do, they love the taste of their food and they refuse to change their diet regardless of the effect it has on their health or environment.

It is understandable that change can be difficult, but changing our diet and producing our food in a sustainable way is an essential step that we must take as a species. The global population is at 7 Billion and growing. To produce enough food to sustain the world population, we cannot depend on the mass production of meat, we are already seeing the damage that the standard American diet is causing and if it continues it will only get worse.

It may not appear to make a difference, but your diet does effect the planet. What we consume, how we consume it, how we produce it – this all has an effect. You may not want to change your ways, but if we want society to change, we need to change.

Chapter 37. Hope for Humanity

"No army can stop an idea whose time has come."
– Victor Hugo

We live in a world that was created from an unlikely series of events. Atoms and molecules formed, and specks of dust created galaxies. Stars and nebulas are destroyed and reborn daily. Our planet was the result of billions of years of astronomical impacts, chemical combinations, and terrestrial evolutions. Human life evolved from molecules of water and developed a unique consciousness; and the forms of life given this amazing gift of life and consciousness, are destroying the very planet from which they were created.

A remarkable chain of events has led to our existence. Earth's thin atmosphere sustains life and is being destroyed by the very life that it is sustaining. We have been given the gift of life and still we take this experience for granted. Unless we realize the effect that we have on our environment, the Earth will become uninhabitable for life, and everything we have ever known, every person, every event, every memory or good feeling we have felt will be nothing but the past of a self-destructive organism.

"A new consciousness is developing which sees the earth as a single organism and recognizes that an organism at war with itself is doomed. We are one planet. One of the great revelations of the age of space exploration is the image of the earth finite and lonely, somehow vulnerable, bearing the entire human species through the oceans of space and time."
– Carl Sagan

To reverse the destruction that we have caused to this planet, we are going to need to contribute a lot—creating projects that utilize natural resources for energy, develop biodegradable waste products, and reduce air pollution—as well as make ourselves more sustainable and less dependent on banks, businesses, and governments.

One of the biggest things we can accomplish is the change to a plant-based diet. Adopting the lifestyle that follows with the change of diet will have a huge impact on our species' health and the health of the planet as a whole. Rather than spending our money on expensive clothes, cars, or electronics, we should be spending our money on organic foods that have the highest nutritional content. We should invest in our family's health rather than the success of environmentally harmful corporations.

We also need to start providing our own resources, growing our own food, and taking the control of our health out of the hands of corporations. To achieve this, we need to return to our sense of community.

Cell phones, computers, and internet have made it so that we can interact with anyone around the world at any moment, but the quality of our relationships around us have become less transparent. We no longer see our neighbors as neighbors, or people as people. We have been taught to look through our eyes and not our hearts. It is critical that humanity strengthens the relationships between people and learns to help each other. We were all born on this planet with no idea of who we are, and are forced to develop based on our surroundings to form a sense of identity, but deep down we are all the same.

With that being said, the thing that will really change the world is not millions of people coming together in acts of retaliation against a corrupt system, but the individuals who learn to liberate themselves from the conditioning of their culture. A system no longer works if we choose to stop participating in it. If there is anything I want you to learn from this book it is that the individual makes up the whole, that everything is interconnected, and without certain pieces to the puzzle you cannot complete the puzzle. Each person makes a difference in what is to come of humanity. We all live on the same Earth, and we all effect the people we come in contact with, in ways we would not imagine.

Each of us has a role to play, and we all need to contribute to making the world a better place. You cannot sit back and do nothing and hope for change; one person can make the biggest difference. Throughout history people have tried to say that we need love and we need to work together, which we do, but you cannot truly love anything unless you learn to love yourself. It all boils down to you, the individual.

When individuals accept themselves, they are liberated from their suffering, and are capable of fully embracing the world around them. You are the only one who can change your life. When the people recognize this, real change will come. Do not wait around for someone else to save the world. You are unique and you have knowledge from your own experience that no one else has. You have ideas and passions that nobody else can claim. You could be the one to help us out of the dreadful situation that we are in, but if you do not act on your ambition the world will never know.

The greatest threat to our planet is the idea that someone else will save it. Once the majority of individuals become aware of themselves and the effect that they have on the world, humanity as a whole will, without a doubt, become a conscious collective.

"We are rare and precious because we are alive, because we can think. We are privileged to influence and perhaps control our future. We have an obligation to fight for life on Earth—not just for ourselves, but for all those, humans and others, who came before us and to whom we are beholden, and for all those who, if we are wise enough, will come after. There is no cause more urgent than to survive to eliminate on a global basis the growing threats of nuclear war, environmental catastrophe, economic collapse and mass starvation. These problems were created by humans and can only be solved by humans. No social convention, no political system, no economic hypothesis, no religious dogma is more important. The hard truth seems to be this: We live in a vast and awesome universe in which, daily, suns are made and worlds destroyed, where humanity clings to an obscure clod of rock. The significance of our lives and our fragile realm derives from our own wisdom and courage. We are the custodians of life's meaning. We would prefer it to be otherwise, of course, but there is no compelling evidence for a cosmic parent who will care for us and save us from ourselves. It is up to us."

– Carl Sagan

"Be the change that you wish to see in the world."

– Mahatma Gandhi